CONTENTS

ACKNOWLEDGEMENTS

My grateful thanks to all who have helped in the growth and development of this work. Special thanks to Norman Welsh who first introduced me to the Folio Text, and to Tina Packer who (with Kristin Linklater and all the members of Shakespeare & Co.) allowed me to explore the texts on the rehearsal floor. To Jane Nichols for her enormous generosity in providing the funding which allowed the material to be computerised. To James and Margaret McBride and Terry Lim for their expertise, good humour and hard work. To the National Endowment for the Arts for their award of a Major Artist Fellowship and to York University for their award of the Joseph G. Green Fellowship. To actors, directors, and dramaturgs at the Stratford Festival, Ontario; Toronto Free Theatre (that was); the Skylight Theatre, Toronto; and Tamanhouse Theatre of Vancouver. To colleagues, friends, and students at The University of British Columbia, Vancouver; York University, Toronto; Concordia University, Montreal; The National Theatre School of Canada in Montreal; Equity Showcase Theatre, Toronto; The Centre for Actors Study and Training (C.A.S.T.), Toronto; The National Voice Intensive at Simon Fraser University, Vancouver; Studio 58 of Langara College, Vancouver; Professional Workshops in the Arts, Vancouver; U.C.L.A., Los Angeles; Loyola Marymount, Los Angeles; San Jose State College, California; Long Beach State College, California; Brigham Young University, Utah and Hawaii; Holy Cross College, Massachusetts; Guilford College, North Carolina. To Chairman John Wright and Associate Dean Don Paterson for their incredible personal support and encouragement. To Rachel Ditor and Tom Scholte for their timely research assistance. To Alan and Chris Baker and Stephanie McWilliams for typographical advice. To Jay L. Halio, Hugh Richmond, and G. B. Shand for their critical input. To the overworked and underpaid proofreading teams of Ron Oten and Yuuattee Tanipersaud, Patrick Galligan and Leslie Barton, Janet Van De Graaff and Angela Dorhman (with input from Todd Sandomirsky, Bruce Alexander Pitkin, Catelyn Thornton, and Michael Roberts). And above all to my wife Julie, for her patient encouragement, courteous advice, critical eye, and long sufferance!

SPECIAL ACKNOWLEDGEMENTS

Glenn Young, Paul Sugarman, and Rachel Reiss of Applause Books; Houghton Mifflin Company for permission to quote from the line numbering system developed for *The Riverside Shakespeare*: Evans, Gwynne Blakemore, Harry Levin, Anne Barton, Herschel Baker, Frank Kermode, Hallet D. Smith, and Marie Edel, editors, *The Riverside Shakespeare*. Copyright © 1974 by Houghton Mifflin Company.

DEFINITIONS OF AND GUIDE TO PHOTOGRAPHIC
COPIES OF THE EARLY TEXTS

(see Appendix A for a brief history of the First Folio, the Quartos,
and their uneasy relationship with modern texts)

A QUARTO (Q)

A single text, so called because of the book size resulting from a particular method of printing. Eighteen of Shakespeare's plays were published in this format by different publishers at various dates between 1594–1622 prior to the appearance of the 1623 Folio. Of the eighteen quarto texts, scholars suggest that fourteen have value as source texts. An extremely useful collection of them is to be found in Michael J. B. Allen and Kenneth Muir, eds., *Shakespeare's Plays in Quarto* (Berkeley: University of California Press, 1981).

THE FIRST FOLIO (F1)[1]

Thirty-six of Shakespeare's plays (excluding *Pericles* and *Two Noble Kinsmen,* in which he had a hand) appeared in one volume published in 1623. All books of this size were termed Folios, again because of the sheet size and printing method, hence this volume is referred to as the First Folio; two recent photographic editions of the work are:

> Charlton Hinman, ed., *The Norton Facsimile (The First Folio of Shakespeare)* (1968; republished New York: W. W. Norton & Company, Inc., 1996).

> Helge Kökeritz, ed., *Mr. William Shakespeare's Comedies, Histories & Tragedies* (New Haven: Yale University Press, 1954).

THE SECOND FOLIO (F2)

Scholars suggest that the Second Folio, dated 1632 but perhaps not published until 1640, has little authority, especially since it created hundreds of new problematical readings of its own. Nevertheless, more than eight hundred modern text readings can be attributed to it. The most recent reproduction is D. S. Brewer, ed., *Mr.*

---

[1] For a full overview of the First Folio see the monumental two-volume work: Charlton Hinman, *The Printing and Proof Reading of the First Folio of Shakespeare* (2 volumes) (Oxford: Clarendon Press, 1963) and W. W. Greg, *The Editorial Problem in Shakespeare: a Survey of the Foundations of the Text,* 3rd. ed. (Oxford: Clarendon Press, 1954); for a brief summary, see the forty-six page publication from Peter W. M. Blayney, *The First Folio of Shakespeare* (Washington, DC: Folger Library Publications, 1991).

William Shakespeare's Comedies, Histories & Tragedies, the Second Folio Reproduced in Facsimile (Dover, NH: Boydell & Brewer Ltd., 1985).

The Third Folio (1664) and the Fourth Folio (1685) have even less authority, and are rarely consulted except in cases of extreme difficulty.

THE THIRD FOLIO (F3)

The Third Folio, carefully proofed (though apparently not against the previous edition) takes great pains to correct anomalies in punctuation ending speeches and in expanding abbreviations. It also introduced seven new plays supposedly written by Shakespeare, only one of which, *Pericles*, has been established as such. The most recent reproduction is D. S. Brewer, ed., *Mr. William Shakespeare's Comedies, Histories & Tragedies, the Third Folio Reproduced in Facsimile* (Dover, NH: Boydell & Brewer Ltd., 1985).

THE FOURTH FOLIO (F4)

Paradoxically, while the Fourth Folio was the most carefully edited of all, its concentration on grammatical clarity and ease of comprehension by its readers at the expense of faithful reproduction of F1 renders it the least useful for those interested in the setting down on paper of Elizabethan theatre texts. The most recent reproduction is D. S. Brewer, ed., *Mr. William Shakespeare's Comedies, Histories & Tragedies, the Fourth Folio Reproduced in Facsimile* (Dover, NH: Boydell & Brewer Ltd., 1985).

WELCOME TO THESE SCRIPTS

These scripts are designed to do three things:

1. show the reader what the First Folio (often referred to as F1) set down on paper, rather than what modern editions think ought to have been set down

2. provide both reader and theatre practitioner an easy journey through some of the information the original readers might have garnered from F1 and other contemporary scripts which is still relevant today

3. provide a simple way for readers to see not only where modern texts alter the First Folio, and how, but also allow readers to explore both First Folio and modern versions of the disputed passage without having to turn to an Appendix or a different text

all this, hopefully without interfering with the action of the play.

What the First Folio sets on paper will be the basis for what you see. In the body of the play-text that follows, the words (including spellings and capitalisations), the punctuation (no matter how ungrammatical), the structure of the lines (including those moments of peculiar verse or unusual prose), the stage directions, the act and scene divisions, and (for the most part) the prefixes used for each character will be as set in the First Folio.

In addition, new, on page, visual symbols specially devised for these texts will help point out both the major stepping stones in the Elizabethan debate/rhetorical process contained in the plays (a fundamental part of understanding both the inner nature of each character as well as the emotional clashes between them), and where and how (and sometimes why) modern texts have altered the First Folio information. And, unlike any other script, opposite each page of text will be a blank page where readers can make their own notes and commentary.

However, there will be the rare occasion when these texts do not exactly follow the First Folio.

Sometimes F1's **words or phrases** are meaningless; for example, the lovely misprinting of 'which' in *Twelfth Night* as 'wh?ch', or in *Romeo and Juliet* the typesetting corruptions of 'speeh' for 'speech' and the running of the two words 'not away' as 'notaway'. If there are no alternative contemporary texts (a Quarto version of the play) or if no modification was made by any of the later Folios (The Second Folio of 1632, The Third Folio of 1664, or The Fourth Folio of 1685, termed F2, F3, and F4 respectively) then the F1 printing will be set as is, no matter how peculiar, and the modern correction footnoted. However, if a more appropriate alternative is available in a Quarto (often referred to as Q) or F2, F3, or F4, that 'correction' will be set directly into the text, replacing the F1 reading, and footnoted accordingly, as in the case of 'wh?ch', 'speeh', and 'notaway'.

The only time F1's **punctuation** will be altered is when the original setting is so blurred that an accurate deciphering of what F1 set cannot be determined. In such cases, alternative punctuation from F2–4 or Q will be set and a footnote will explain why.

The only time F1's **line structure** will not be followed is when at the end of a very long line, the final word or part of the word cannot fit onto the single line, nor be set as a new line in F1 because of the text that follows and is therefore set above or below the original line at the right hand side of the column. In such rare cases these texts will complete the line as a single line, and mark it with a † to show the change from F1. In all other cases, even when in prose F1 is forced to split the final word of a speech in half, and set only a few letters of it on a new line—for example in *Henry the Fifth*, Pistoll's name is split as 'Pi' on one line and 'stoll' (as the last part of the speech) on the next—these texts will show F1 exactly as set.

Some liberties have to be taken with the **prefixes** (the names used at the beginning of speeches to show the reader which character is now speaking), for Ff (all the Folios) and Qq (all the Quartos) are not always consistent. Sometimes slightly different abbreviations are used for the same character—in *The Tempest*, King Alonso is variously referred to as 'Al.', 'Alo.', 'Alon.', and 'Alonso'. Sometimes the same abbreviation is used for two different characters—in *A Midsummer Nights Dream* the characters Quince, the 'director' and author of the Mechanicals play, and Titania, Queen of the fairies, are given the same abbreviation 'Qu.'. While in this play common sense can distinguish what is intended, the confusions in *Julius Caesar* between Lucius and Lucullus, each referred to sometimes as 'Luc.', and in *The Comedy of Errors,* where the twin brothers Antipholus are both abbreviated to 'Antiph.', cannot be so easily sorted out. Thus, whereas F1 will show a variety of abbreviated prefixes, these texts will usually choose just one complete name per character and stay with it throughout.

However, there are certain cases where one full name will not suffice. Sometimes F1 will change the prefix for a single character from scene to scene, the change usually reflecting the character's new function or status. Thus in *The Comedy of Errors,* as a drinking companion of the local Antipholus, the goldsmith Angelo is referred to by his given name 'Ang.', but once business matters go awry he very quickly becomes a businessman, referred to as 'Gold'. Similar changes affect most of the characters in *A Midsummer Nights Dream,* and a complex example can be found in *Romeo and Juliet.* While modern texts give Juliet's mother the single prefix Lady Capulet throughout (incorrectly since neither she nor Capulet are named as aristocrats anywhere in the play) both Ff and Qq refer to her in a wonderful character-revealing multiplicity of ways—Mother, Capulet Wife, Lady, and Old Lady—a splendid gift for actress, director, designer, and reader alike.

Surprisingly, no modern text ever sets any of these variations. Believing such changes integral to the development of the characters so affected, these texts will. In such cases, each time the character's prefix changes the new prefix will be set, and a small notation alongside the prefix (either by reference to the old name, or by adding the symbol •) will remind the reader to whom it refers.

Also, some alterations will be made to F1's **stage directions,** not to the words themselves or when they occur, but to the way they are going to be presented visually. Scholars agree F1 contains two different types of stage direction: those that came in the original manuscript from which the Playhouse copy of the play was made, and a second set that were added in for theatrical clarification by the Playhouse. The scholars conjecture that the literary or manuscript directions, presumably from Shakespeare, mainly dealing with entries and key actions such as battles, are those that F1 sets centred on a separate line, while the additional Playhouse directions, usually dealing with offstage sounds, music, and exits, are those F1 sets alongside the spoken dialogue, usually flush against the right hand side of the column. In performance terms there seems to be a useful distinction between the two, though this is only a rule of thumb. The centred manuscript (Shakespearean?) directions tend to stop or change the action of the play, that is, the scene is affected by the action the direction demands, whereas the Playhouse directions (to the side of the text) serve to underscore what is already taking place. (If a word is needed to distinguish the two, the centred directions can be called 'action' directions, because they are events in and of themselves, while the side-set directions could be called 'supportive' or 'continuous' since they tend not to distract from the current onstage action.)

Since F1 seems to visually distinguish between the two types (setting them on different parts of the page) and there seems to be a logical theatrical differentiation as to both the source and function of each, it seems only appropriate that these scripts also mark the difference between them. Both Ff and Qq's side-set directions are often difficult to decipher while reading the text: sometimes they are set so close to the spoken text they get muddled up with it, despite the different typeface, and oftentimes have to be abbreviated to fit in. These are drawbacks shared by most modern texts. Thus these texts will distinguish them in a slightly different way (see p. xxvi below).

Finally, there will be two occasional alterations to Ff's **fonts.** F1 used **italics** for a large number of different purposes, sometimes creating confusion on the page. What these texts will keep as italics are letters, poems, songs, and the use of foreign languages. What they will not set in italics are real names, prefixes, and stage directions. Also at the top of each play, and sometimes at the beginning of a letter or poem, F1 would set a large wonderfully **decorative opening letter,** with the second letter of the word being capitalised, the style tying in with the borders that surrounded the opening and closing of each play. Since these texts will not be reproducing the decorative borders, the decorative letters won't be set either.

MAKING FULL USE OF THESE TEXTS

WHAT MODERN CHANGES WILL BE SHOWN

WORDS AND PHRASES

Modern texts often tidy up F1's words and phrases. Real names, both of people and places, and foreign languages are often reworked for modern understanding; for example, the French town often set in F1 as 'Callice' is usually reset as 'Calais'. Modern texts 'correct' the occasional Elizabethan practice of setting a singular noun with plural verb (and vice versa), as well as the infrequent use of the past tense of a verb to describe a current situation. These texts will set the F1 reading, and footnote the modern corrections whenever they occur.

More problematical are the possibilities of choice, especially when a Q and F version of the same play show a different reading for the same line and either choice is valid—even more so when both versions are offered by different modern texts. Juliet's 'When I shall die,/Take him and cut him out in little starres' offered by Ff/Q1-3 being offset by Q4's 'When he shall die...' is a case in point. Again, these texts will set the F1 reading, and footnote the alternatives.

LINE STRUCTURE CHANGES RELATED TO PROBLEMS OF 'CASTING-OFF'

The First Folio was usually prepared in blocks of twelve pages at a time. Six pairs of pages would be prepared, working both forward and backward simultaneously. Thus from the centre of any twelve-page block, pages six and seven were set first, then five and eight, then four and nine, then three and ten, then two and eleven, and finally one and twelve. This meant each compositor had to work out very carefully how much copy would fit not only each sheet, but also how much would be needed overall to reach the outer edges of pages one and twelve to match it to the previously set text, (prior to page one) or about to be set text (after page twelve). Naturally the calculations weren't always accurate. Sometimes there was too little text left for too great a space: in such cases, if the manuscript were set as it should have been, a great deal of empty paper would be left free, a condition often described as 'white' space. Sometimes too much text remained for too small a space, and if the manuscript were to be set according to its normal layout, every available inch would be taken up with type (and even then the text might not fit), a condition that could be described as 'crammed space'.

Essentially, this created a huge design problem, and most commentators suggest when it arose the printing house policy was to sacrifice textual accuracy to neatness of design. Thus, so the argument goes, in the case of white space, extra lines of type would have to be created where (presumably) none originally existed. *Hamlet* provides an excellent example with the Polonius speech 'Indeed that's out of the air' starting at line 78 of what most modern texts term Act Two Scene 2. Q2 sets the four-line speech as prose, and most modern texts follow suit. However, F1, faced with a potentially huge white space problem at the bottom of the right hand column of p. 261 in the Tragedy section, resets the speech as eleven lines of very irregular verse! In the case of crammed space, five lines of verse might suddenly become three lines of prose, or in one very severe case of overcrowding in *Henry The Fourth Part Two,* words, phrases, and even half lines of text might be omitted to reduce the text sufficiently.

When such cases occur, this text will set F1 as shown, and the modern texts' suggested alternatives will be footnoted and discussed.

LINE STRUCTURE CHANGES NOT RELATED TO PROBLEMS OF 'CASTING-OFF'

In addition, modern texts regularly make changes to F1's line structure which are not related to 'white' or 'crammed' space, often to the detriment of both character and scene. Two major reasons are offered for the changes.

First, either (a few) prose lines suddenly appear in what essentially is a verse scene (or a few verse lines in a sea of prose) and the modern texts, feeling the scene should be standardised, restructure the offending lines accordingly. *The Tempest* is atrociously served this way[2], for where F1, the only source text, shows the conspirators Caliban, Stephano, and, very occasionally, Trinculo, speaking verse as well as prose even within the same speech (a sure sign of personal striving and inner disturbance) most modern texts readjust the lines to show only Caliban speaking verse (dignifying him more than he deserves) and Stephano and Trinculo only speaking prose (thus robbing them of their dangerous flights of fancy).

Second, some Ff verse lines appear so appallingly defective in terms of their rhythm and length that modern texts feel it necessary to make a few 'readjustments' of the lines around them to bring the offending lines back to a coherent, rhythmic whole. Many of the later plays are abominably served in this regard: in *Macbeth,* for example, over a hundred F1 passages involving more than 200 lines (90 percent of which were set by the usually reliable compositor A) have been altered by most modern texts. Most of these changes concentrate on regularising moments where a character is under tremendous upheaval and hardly likely to be speaking pure formal verse at that particular moment!

These changes come about through a mistaken application of modern grammat-

---

[2] Commentators suggest the copy play used for setting F1, coming from Stratford as it did, and thus unsupervised by Shakespeare in the Playhouse preparation of the document, prepared by Ralph Crane, was at times defective, especially in distinguishing clearly between verse and prose: this is why most modern texts do not follow F1's choices in these dubious passages: readers are invited to explore *The Tempest* within this series, especially the footnotes, as a theatrical vindication of the original F1 setting

ical considerations to texts that were originally prepared not according to grammar but rhetoric. One of rhetoric's many strengths is that it can show not only when characters are in self-control but also when they are not. In a rhetorically set passage, the splutters of a person going through an emotional breakdown, as with Othello, can be shown almost verbatim, with peculiar punctuations, spellings, breaks, and all. If the same passage were to be set grammatically it would be very difficult to show the same degree of personal disintegration on the printed page.[3] F1's occasional weird shifts between verse and prose and back again, together with the moments of extreme linear breakdown, are the equivalents of human emotional breakdown, and once the anomalies of Elizabethan script preparation are accounted for,[4] the rhetorical breakdowns on F1's printed page are clear indications of a character's disintegration within the play. When modern texts tidy up such blemishes grammatically they unwittingly remove essential theatrical and/or character clues for reader and theatre person alike.

In these texts, F1's line structure will be set as is, and all such modern alterations (prose to verse, verse to prose, regularisation of originally unmetrical lines) will be shown. The small symbol ° will be added to show where modern texts suggest a line should end rather than where F1 shows it does. A thin vertical line will be set to the left alongside any text where the modern texts have converted F1's prose to verse, or vice versa. The more large-scale of these changes will be boxed for quicker reader recognition. Most of these changes will be footnoted in the text where they occur, and a comparison of the two different versions of the text and what each could signify theatrically will be offered. For examples of both, see p. xxiii below.

THE SPECIAL PROBLEMS AFFECTING WHAT ARE KNOWN AS 'SHARED' OR 'SPLIT' VERSE LINES

A definition, and their importance to the Shakespeare texts

Essentially, split lines are short lines of verse which, when placed together, form the equivalent of a full verse line. Most commentators suggest they are very useful in speeding the play along, for the second character (whose line attaches on to the end of the first short line) is expected to use the end of the first character's line as a

---

[3] For a full discussion of this, readers are directed to Neil Freeman, *Shakespeare's First Texts* (Vancouver: Folio Scripts, 1994).

[4] Readers are referred to an excellent chapter by Gary Taylor which analyses the whole background, conjectured and known, concerning the preparation of the first scripts. He points out the pitfalls of assuming the early texts as sole authority for all things Shakespearean: he examines the conjectured movement of the scripts from Shakespeare's pen to printed edition, and carefully examples the changes and alterations that could occur, (most notably at the hands of the manuscript copyists), as well as the interferences and revampings of the Playhouse, plus the effects of the first typesetters' personal habits and carelessness. Stanley Wells and Gary Taylor, *William Shakespeare: A Textual Companion* (Oxford: Clarendon Press, 1987), 1–68.

springboard and jump in with an immediate reply, enhancing the quickness of the debate. Thus in *Measure for Measure*, Act Two Scene 2, modern ll. 8–10, the Provost, trying to delay Claudio's execution, has asked Angelo whether Claudio has to die the following day: Angelo's questioning affirmation ends with a very pointed short line, followed immediately by a short line opening from the Provost.

Angelo	Did I not tell thee yea? hadst thou not order?
	Why do'st thou aske againe?
Provost	Lest I might be too rash:
	Under your good correction, I have seene
	When after execution . . .

If the Provost replies immediately after, or just as, Angelo finishes, an explosive dramatic tension is created. Allowing a minor delay before reply, as many actors do, will reduce the impact of the moment, and create a hesitation where one probably does not exist.

The occasional problem

So far so good. But the problems start when more than two short lines follow each other. If there are three short lines in succession, which should be joined, #1 and #2, or #2 and #3? Later in the same scene, Claudio's sister Isabella has, at the insistence of Claudio's friend Lucio, come to plead with Angelo for her brother's life. In Lucio's eyes she is giving up too easily, hence the following (modern ll. 45–49):

Lucio	You are too cold: if you should need a pin,
	You could not with more tame a tongue desire it:
	To him, I say.
Isabella	Must he needs die?
Angelo	Maiden, no remedie?

And here it seems fairly obvious Isabella and Angelo's lines should join together, thus allowing a wonderful dramatic pause following Lucio's urging before Isabella plucks up enough courage to try. Most modern texts set the lines accordingly, with Lucio's the short odd line out.

But what about the three lines contained in the exchange that follows almost straightaway?

Isabella	But you might doe't & do the world no wrong
	If so your heart were touch'd with that remorse,
	As mine is to him?
Angelo	Hee's sentenc'd, tis too late.
Lucio	You are too cold.
Isabella	Too late? why no: I that doe speak a word

>   May call it againe: well, beleeve this
>   (modern line numbering 53–56)

Does Angelo's 'Hee's sentenc'd...' spring off Isabella's line, leaving Isabella speechless and turning to go before Lucio urges her on again? Or does Angelo pause (to frame a reply?) before speaking, leaving Lucio to quickly jump in quietly giving Isabella no time to back off? Either choice is possible, and dramatically valid. And readers should be allowed to make their own choice, which automatically means each reader should able to see the possibility of such choices when they occur.

The problem magnified by the way modern texts set split/shared lines

However, because of a peculiarity faced by the modern texts not shared by Ff/Qq, modern texts rarely show such possibilities to their readers but make the choice for them. The peculiarity comes about from a change in text layout initiated in the eighteenth century.

Ff/Qq always set short lines directly under one another, as shown in the examples above. In 1778 George Steevens, a highly respected editor, started to show split lines a new way, by advancing the second split line to just beyond where the first split line finishes, viz.

> Angelo   Did I not tell thee yea? hadst thou not order?
>   Why do'st thou aske againe?
>
> Provost   Lest I might be too rash:
>   Under your good correction, I have seene
>   When after execution ...

Since that date all editions of Shakespeare have followed this practice, which is fine as long as there are only two short lines, but when three follow each other, a choice has to be made. Thus the second Isabella/Angelo/Lucio sequence could be set as either

> Isabella   But you might doe't & do the world no wrong
>   If so your heart were touch'd with that remorse,
>   As mine is to him?
>
> Angelo   Hee's sentenc'd, tis too late.
>
> Lucio   You are too cold.
>
> Isabella   Too late? why no: I that doe speak a word
>   May call it againe: well, beleeve this ...

(the usual modern choice), or

> Isabella   But you might doe't & do the world no wrong
>   If so your heart were touch'd with that remorse,
>   As mine is to him?

Angelo	Hee's sentenc'd, tis too late.
Lucio	You are too cold.
Isabella	Too late? why no: I that doe speak a word
	May call it againe: well, beleeve this . . .

This modern typesetting convention has robbed the reader of a very important moment of choice. Indeed, at the beginning of the twentieth century, Richard Flatter[5] suggested that what modern commentators consider to be split lines may not be split lines at all. He offers two other suggestions: pauses and hesitations could exist between each line, or the lines could in fact be spoken one on top of another, a very important consideration for the crowd responses to Anthony in the funeral scene of *Julius Caesar*. Either way, the universally adopted Steevens layout precludes the reader/theatre practitioner from even seeing such possibilities.

These texts will show the F1 layout as is, and will indicate via footnote when a choice is possible (in the case of three short lines, or more, in succession) and by the symbol } when the possibility of springboarding exists. Thus the Folio Texts would show the first Angelo/Provost example as:

Angelo	Did I not tell thee yea? hadst thou not order?
	Why do'st thou aske againe?
	}
Provost	Lest I might be too rash:
	Under your good correction, I have seene
	When after execution . . .

In nearly all cases the } shows where most modern texts insist on setting a shared split line. However, readers are cautioned that in many of the later plays, the single line so created is much longer than pentameter, and often very a-rhythmic. In such cases the lines could have great value as originally set (two separate short lines), especially when a key debate is in process (for example, *Measure for Measure, The Tragedie of Cymbeline, Othello,* and *The Winters Tale*).

The Unusual Single Split Line (please see 'a caveat', p. xxxviii)

So far the discussion has centred on short lines shared by two or more characters. Ff/Qq offer another complication rarely, if ever, accepted by most modern texts. Quite often, and not because of white space, a single character will be given two consecutive short lines within a single speech. *Romeo and Juliet* is chock full of this device: in the famous balcony scene (modern texts numbering 2.2.62–3) Juliet asks Romeo

How cam'st thou hither.

---

5   Richard Flatter, *Shakespeare's Producing Hand* (London: Heinemann, 1948, reprint).

> Tell me, and wherefore?
> The Orchard walls are high, and hard to climbe

The first two lines (five syllables each) suggest a minute pause between them as Juliet hesitates before asking the all important second line (with its key second part 'and wherefore'). Since Qq rarely set such 'single split lines' most modern texts refuse to set any of them, but combine them:

> How cams't thou hither. Tell me and wherefore?

This basically F1 device is set by all the compositors and followed by all other Folios. This text will follow suit, highlighting them with the symbol → for quick recognition, viz.:

> How cam'st thou hither. →
> Tell me, and wherefore?
> The Orchard walls are high, and hard to climbe

SENTENCE AND PUNCTUATION STRUCTURES

A CHARACTER'S THOUGHTFUL & EMOTIONAL JOURNEY

A quick comparison between these texts and both the Ff/Qq's and the modern texts will reveal two key differences in the layout of the dialogue on the printed page — the bolding of major punctuation, and the single line dropping of text whenever a new sentence begins.

The underlying principle behind these texts is that since the handwritten documents from which they stem were originally intended for the actor and Playhouse, in addition to their poetical values, the Ff/Qq scripts represent a theatrical process. Even if the scripts are being read just for pleasure, at the back of the reader's mind should be the notion of characters on a stage and actors acting (and the word 'process' rather than 'practice' is deliberate, with process suggesting a progression, development, or journey).

The late Jean-Louis Barrault gave a wonderful definition of acting, and of this journey, suggesting an actor's job was to strive to remain in 'the ever-changing present'. If something happens onstage (an entry, an exit, a verbal acceptance or denial of what the actor's character has suggested), the 'present' has changed, and the character must readjust accordingly. Just as onstage, the actor should be prepared for the character to re-adjust, and in rehearsal should be examining how and why it does, so should the reader in the library, armchair, or classroom.

In many ways, the key to Shakespeare is discovering how each character's mind works; perceiving the emotions and intellects as they act and react helps the reader understand from where the poetical imagination and utterance stem.

Certain elements of each character's emotional and intellectual journey, and where it changes, are encoded into the sentence structure of Ff/Qq.

Elizabethan education prepared any schooled individual (via the 'petty school' and the private tutor) for the all important and essential daily rough and tumble of argument and debate. Children were trained not only how to frame an argument so as to win it hands down, but also how to make it entertaining so as to enthrall the neutral listener.

The overall training, known as 'rhetoric', essentially allowed intellect and emotion to exist side by side, encouraging the intellect to keep the emotion in check. The idea was not to deny the emotions, but ensure they didn't swamp the 'divinity' of reason, the only thing separating man from beast. While the initial training was mainly vocal, any written matter of the period automatically reflected the ebb and flow of debate. What was set on the printed page was not grammar, but a representation of the rhetorical process.

DROPPING A LINE TO ILLUSTRATE F1'S SENTENCE STRUCTURE

Put at its simplest, in any document of the period, each sentence would represent a new intellectual and emotional stage of a rhetorical argument. When this stage of the argument was completed, a period would be set (occasionally a question mark or, much more rarely, an exclamation mark — both followed by a capital letter) signifying the end of that stage of the argument, and the beginning of the next.

Thus in the First Folio, the identification of each new sentence is an automatic (and for us, four hundred years later, a wonderful) aid to understanding how a character is reacting to and dealing with Barrault's ever-changing present.

To help the reader quickly spot the new steppingstone in an argument, and thus the point of transition, these texts highlight where one sentence ends and the new one begins by simply dropping a line whenever a new sentence starts. Thus the reader has a visual reminder that the character is making a transition to deal with a change in the current circumstances of the scene (or in the process of self-discovery in the case of soliloquies).

This device has several advantages. The reader can instantly see where the next step in the argument begins. The patterns so created on the page can quickly illuminate whenever a contrast between characters' thought patterns occurs. (Sometimes the sentences are short and precise, suggesting the character is moving quickly from one idea to the next. Sometimes the sentences are very long, suggesting the character is undergoing a very convoluted process. Sometimes the sentences contain nothing but facts, suggesting the character has no time to entertain; sometimes they are filled with high-flown imagery, perhaps suggesting the character is trying to mask a very weak argument with verbal flummery.) The patterns can also show when a character's style changes within itself, say from long and convoluted to short and precise, or vice versa. It can also immediately pinpoint when a character is in trouble and not arguing coherently or logically, something modern texts often alter out of grammatical necessity.

With patience, all this could be gleaned from the modern texts (in as far as they set the Ff sentence structure, which they often don't) and from a photostat of the First Folio, by paying special attention to where the periods are set. But there is one extra very special advantage to this new device of dropping a line: this has to do once more with the Elizabethan method of setting down spoken argument on paper, especially when the character speaking is not in the best of all possible worlds.

If an Elizabethan person/character is arguing well, neatly, cleanly, tidily, then a printed representation of that argument would also be clean, neat, and tidy—to modern eyes it would be grammatically acceptable. If the same character is emotionally upset, or incapable of making a clear and tidy argument, then the on-paper representation would be muddy and untidy—to modern eyes totally ungrammatical and often not acceptable. By slightly isolating each sentence these texts very quickly allow the reader to spot when a sentence's construction is not all that it should be, say in the middle of Viola's so-called ring speech in *Twelfth Night* (Act Two Scene 2), or Helena's declaration of love for Bertram in *All's Well That Ends Well* (Act One Scene 3), or the amazing opening to *As You Like It,* where Orlando's opening litany of complaint against his brother starts with a single sentence twenty lines long.

This is especially relevant when a surprising modern editorial practice is accounted for. Very often the Ff sentence structures are markedly altered by modern texts, especially when the Ff sentences do not seem 'grammatical'—thus Orlando's twenty-line monster is split into six separate, grammatically correct sentences by all modern texts. And then there is the case of Shylock in *The Merchant of Venice,* a Jewish man being goaded and tormented beyond belief by the very Christians who helped his daughter elope with a Christian, taking a large part of Shylock's fortune with her. A sentence comparison of the famous Act Three Scene 1 speech culminating in 'Hath not a Jew eyes?' is very instructive. All modern texts set the speech as between fifteen and seventeen sentences in length: whatever the pain, anger, and personal passion, the modern texts encourage dignity and self-control, a rational Shylock. But this is a Shylock completely foreign to both Q1 and Ff. Q1 show the same speech as only four sentences long, Ff five—a veritable onflow of intellect and passion all mixed together, all unstoppable for the longest period of time—a totally different being from that shown by the modern texts. What is more, this is a totally different Shylock from the one seen earlier in the Ff/Q1 version of the play, where, even in the extremes of discomfort with the old enemy Anthonio, his sentence structures are rhetorically balanced and still grammatical to modern eyes.

Here, with Shylock, there are at least three benefits to dropping the sentence: the unusualness of the speech is immediately spotted; the change in style between this and any of his previous speeches can be quickly seen; and, above all, the moment where the speech moves from a long unchecked outpouring to a quick series of brief, dangerously rational sentences can be quickly identified. And these advantages will be seen in such changed sentence circumstances in any play in any of these texts.

THE HIGHLIGHTING OF THE MAJOR PUNCTUATION IN THESE TEXTS

A second key element of rhetoric encoded into the Ff/Qq texts clearly shows the characters' mind in action. The encoding lies in the remaining punctuation which, unlike much modern punctuation, serves a double function, one dealing with the formation of the thought, the other with the speaking of it.

Apart from the period, dealt with already, essentially there are two sets of punctuation to consider, minor and major, each with their own very specific functions.

Shakespearean characters reflect the mode of thinking of their time. Elizabethans were trained to constantly add to or modify thoughts. They added a thought to expand the one already made. They denied the first thought so as to set up alternatives. They elaborated a thought so as to clarify what has already been said. They suddenly moved into splendid puns or non-sequiturs (emotional, logical, or both) because they had been immediately stimulated by what they or others had just said. The **minor punctuation** (essentially the comma [,] the parenthesis or bracket [( )], and the dash) reflects all this.

In establishing thought processes for each character, minor punctuation shows every new nuance of thought: every tiny punctuation in this category helps establish the deftness and dance of each character's mind. In *As You Like It* (Act Three Scene 2, modern line numbering 400–402) the Ff setting of Rosalind's playing with her beloved Orlando has a wonderful coltish exuberance as she runs rings round his protestations of love:

> Love is meerely a madnesse, and I tel you,
> deserves as well a darke house,* and a whip,* as madmen do:

Her mind is adding extra thoughts as she goes: the Ff commas are as much part of her spirit and character as the words are—though most modern texts create a much more direct essayist, preaching what she already knows, by removing the two Ff commas marked *.[6]

A similar situation exists with Macbeth, facing Duncan whom he must kill if he is

---

[6]   Unfortunately, many modern texts eradicate the F and Q minor punctuation arguing the need for light (or infrequent) punctuation to preserve the speed of speech. This is not necessarily helpful, since what it removes is just a new thought marker, not an automatic indication to pause: too often the result is that what the first texts offer a character as a series of closely-worked out dancing thought-patterns (building one quick thought—as marked by a comma—on top of another) is turned into a series of much longer phrases: often, involved and reactive busy minds are artificially turned into (at best) eloquent ones, suddenly capable of perfect and lengthy rationality where the situation does not warrant such a reaction, or (at worst) vapid ones, speaking an almost preconceived essay of commentary or artificial sentimentality.

to become king (Act One Scene 4, modern line numbering 22–27). Ff show a
Macbeth almost swamped with extra thoughts as he assures Duncan

> The service,* and the loyaltie I owe,
> In doing it,* payes it selfe.
> Your highnesse part,* is to receive our Duties,
> And our Duties are to your Throne,* and State,
> Children,* and Servants; which doe but what they should,*
> By doing every thing safe toward your Love
> And Honour.

The heavy use of minor punctuation—especially when compared with most
modern texts which remove the commas marked *, leaving Macbeth with just six
thoughts compared to Ff's twelve—clearly shows a man ill at ease and/or working
too hard to say the right thing. Again the punctuation helps create an understanding
of the character.

However, while the minor punctuation is extremely important in the discovery
process of reading and/or rehearsal, paradoxically, it mustn't become too dominant.
From the performance/speaking viewpoint, to pause at each comma would be tan-
tamount to disaster. There would be an enormous dampening effect if reader/actor
were to pause at every single piece of punctuation: the poetry would be destroyed
and the event would become interminable.

In many ways, minor punctuation is the Victorian child of Shakespearean texts,
it must be seen but not heard. (In speaking the text, the new thought the minor
punctuation represents can be added without pausing: a change in timbre, rhythm,
or pitch—in acting terms, occurring naturally with changes in intention—will do the
trick.)

But once thoughts have been discovered, they have to be organised into some
form of coherent whole. If the period shows the end of one world and the start of
the new, and if the comma marks a series of small, ever-changing, ever-evolving
thoughts within each world, occasionally there must be pause for reflection somewhere in the helter-skelter of tumbling new ideas. This is the **major punctuation's**
strength; major punctuation consisting of the semicolon [;], and the colon [:].

Major punctuation marks the gathering together of a series of small thoughts
within an overall idea before moving onto something new. If a room full of Rodin
sculptures were analogous to an Elizabethan scene or act, each individual piece of
sculpture would be a speech, the torso or back or each major limb a separate sentence. Each collective body part (a hand, the wrist, the forearm, the upper arm)
would be a series of small thoughts bounded by major punctuation, each smaller
item within that part (a finger, a fingernail, a knuckle) a single small thought separated by commas. In describing the sculpture to a friend one might move from the
smaller details (the knuckle) to the larger (the hand) to another larger (the wrist)

then another (the forearm) and so on to the whole limb. Unless the speaker is emotionally moved by the recollection, some pauses would be essential, certainly after finishing the whole description of the arm (the sentence), and probably after each major collective of the hand, the wrist, etc. (as marked by the major punctuation), but not after every small bit.

As a rule of thumb, and simply stated, the colon and semicolon mark both a thinking and a speaking pause. The vital difference between major and minor punctuation, whether in the silent reading of the text or the performing of it aloud, is you need not pause at the comma, bracket, or dash; you probably should at the colon, semicolon, and period.

Why the Major Punctuation is Bolded in These Texts.

In speaking the text or reading it, the minor punctuation indicates the need to key onto the new thought without necessarily requiring a pause. In so doing, the inherent rhythms of speech, scene, and play can clip along at the rate suggested by the Prologue in *Romeo and Juliet,* 'the two hours traffic of the stage', until a pause is absolutely necessary. Leave the commas alone, and the necessary pauses will make themselves known.

The 'major' punctuation then comes into its own, demanding double attention as both a thinking and speaking device. This is why it is bolded, to highlight it for the reader's easier access. The reader can still use all the punctuation when desired, working through the speech thought by thought, taking into account both major and minor punctuation as normal. Then, when needed, the bolding of the major punctuation will allow the reader easy access for marking where the speech, scene, or play needs to be broken down into its larger thinking/speaking (and even breathing) units without affecting its overall flow.

The Blank Pages Within the Text

In each text within this series, once readers reach the play itself they will find that with each pair of pages the dialogue is printed on the right-hand page only. The left-hand page has been deliberately left blank so that readers, actors, directors, stage managers, teachers, etc. have ample space for whatever notes and text emendations they may wish to add.

PRACTICAL ON-PAGE HELP FOR THE READER

THE VISUAL SYMBOLS HIGHLIGHTING MODERN ALTERATIONS

THE BOX

This surrounds a passage where the modern texts have made whole-scale alterations to the Ff text. Each boxed section will be footnoted, and the changes analysed at the bottom of the page.

THE FOOTNOTES

With many modern texts the footnotes are not easily accessible. Often no indication is given within the text itself where the problem/choice/correction exists. Readers are forced into a rather cumbersome four-step process. First, they have to search through the bottom of the page where the footnotes are crammed together, often in very small print, to find a line number where an alteration has been made. Then they must read the note to find out what has been altered. Then they must go back to the text and search the side of the page to find the corresponding line number. Having done all this, finally they can search the line to find the word or phrase that has been changed (sometimes complicated by the fact the word in question is set twice in different parts of the line).

These texts will provide a reference marker within the text itself, directly alongside the word or phrase that is in question. This guides the reader directly to the corresponding number in the footnote section of the bottom of each page, to the alteration under discussion—hopefully a much quicker and more immediate process.

In addition, since there are anywhere between 300 and 1,100 footnotes in any one of these texts, a tool is offered to help the reader find only those notes they require, when they require them. In the footnote section, prior to the number that matches the footnote marker in the text, a letter or combination of letters will be set as a code. The letter 'W', for example, shows that the accompanying footnote refers to word substitutions offered by modern texts; the letters 'SD' refer to an added or altered stage direction; the letters 'LS' show the footnote deals with a passage where the modern texts have completely altered the line-structure that F1 set. This enables readers to be selective when they want to examine only certain changes, for they can quickly skim through the body of footnotes until they find the code they want, perhaps those dealing with changes in prefixes (the code 'P') or when modern alterations have been swapping lines from verse to prose or vice versa (the code 'VP'). For full details of the codes, see pp. xxxiii–xxxv below.

Readers are urged to make full use of the footnotes in any of the Recommended Texts listed just before the start of the play. They are excellent in their areas of expertise. To attempt to rival or paraphrase them would be redundant. Thus the foot-notes in these scripts will hardly ever deal with word meanings and derivations; so-cial or political history; literary derivations and comparisons; or lengthy quotations from scholars or commentators. Such information is readily available in the *Oxford English Dictionary* and from the recommended modern texts.

Generally, the footnotes in these scripts will deal with matters theatrical and tex-tual and will be confined to three major areas: noting where and how the modern texts alter F1's line structure; showing popular alternative word readings often selected by the modern texts (these scripts will keep the F1 reading unless otherwise noted); and showing the rare occasions where and how these scripts deviate from their source texts. When the modern texts offer alternative words and/or phrases to F2-4/Qq, the original spelling and punctuation will be used. Where appropriate, the footnotes will briefly refer to the excellent research of the scholars of the last three centuries, and to possible theatrical reasons for maintaining F1's structural 'irregularities'.

THE SYMBOL °

This will be used to show where modern texts have altered F1's line structure, and will allow the reader to explore both the F1 setting and the modern alternative while examining the speech where it is set, in its proper context and rightful position within the play. For example, though F1 is usually the source text for *Henry the Fifth* and sets the dialogue for Pistoll in prose, most modern texts use the memorial Q version and change his lines to (at times extraordinarily peculiar) verse. These texts will set the speech as shown in F1, but add the ° to show the modern texts alterations, thus:

> Pistoll   Fortune is Bardolphs foe, and frownes on him:°
> for he hath stolne a Pax, and hanged must a be:° a damned
> death:° let Gallowes gape for Dogge, let Man goe free,°
> and let not Hempe his Wind-pipe suffocate:° but Exeter
> hath given the doome of death,° for Pax of little price.°
>
> Therefore goe speake,° the Duke will heare thy voyce;°
> and let not Bardolphs vitall thred bee cut° with edge of
> Penny-Cord, and vile reproach.°
>   Speake Captaine for
> his Life, and I will thee requite.°
>   (*Henry V*, These Scripts, 2.1.450–459)

Read the speech utilising the ° to mark the end of a line, and the reader is ex-ploring what the modern texts suggest should be the structure. Read the lines ig-noring the ° and the reader is exploring what the F1 text really is. Thus both F1 and modern/Q versions can be read within the body of the text.

THE VERTICAL LINE TO THE LEFT OF THE TEXT

This will be used to mark a passage where modern editors have altered F1's verse to prose or vice versa. Here is a passage in a predominantly prose scene from *Henry V*. Modern texts and F1 agree that Williams and Fluellen should be set in prose. However, the F1 setting for Henry could be in verse, though most modern texts set it in prose too. The thin vertical line to the left of the text is a quick reminder to the reader of disagreement between Ff and modern texts (the F1 setting will always be shown, and the disputed section will be footnoted accordingly).

> King Henry   Twas I indeed thou promised'st to strike,
>   And thou hast given me most bitter termes.
>
> Fluellen   And please your Majestie, let his Neck answere
>   for it, if there is any Marshall Law in the World.
>
> King Henry   How canst thou make me satisfaction?
>
> Williams   All offences, my Lord, come from the heart: ne-
>   ver came any from mine, that might offend your Ma-
>   jestie.   (*Henry V,* These Scripts, 4.1.240–247)

THE SYMBOL } SET TO THE RIGHT OF TEXT, CONNECTING TWO SPEECHES

This will be used to remind readers of the presence of what most modern texts consider to be split or shared lines, and that therefore the second speech could springboard quickly off the first, thus increasing the speed of the dialogue and debate; for example:

> Angelo   Did I not tell thee yea? hadst thou not order?
>   Why do'st thou ask againe?
>   }
> Provost   Lest I might be too rash:
>   Under your good correction, I have seene
>   When after execution . . .

Since there is no definitive way of determining whether Shakespeare wished the two short lines to be used as a shared or split line, or used as two separate short lines, the reader would do well to explore the moment twice. The first time the second speech could be 'springboarded' off the first as if it were a definite shared line; the second time round a tiny break could be inserted before speaking the second speech, as if a hesitation were deliberately intended. This way both possibilities of the text can be examined.

THE SYMBOL → TO THE RIGHT OF THE TEXT, JOINING TWO SHORT LINES SPOKEN BY A SINGLE CHARACTER

This indicates that though Ff has set two short lines for a single character, perhaps hinting at a minute break between the two thoughts, most modern texts have set the two short lines as one longer one. Thus the first two lines of Juliet's

> How cam'st thou hither. →

> Tell me, and wherefore?
> The Orchard walls are high, and hard to climbe

can be explored as one complete line (the interpretation of most modern texts), or, as F1 suggests, as two separate thoughts with a tiny hesitation between them. In most cases these lines will be footnoted, and possible reasons for the F1 interpretation explored.

THE OCCASIONAL USE OF THE †

This marks where F1 has been forced, in a crowded line, to set the end of the line immediately above or below the first line, flush to the right hand column. These texts will set the original as one complete line—the only instance where these scripts do not faithfully reproduce F1's line structure.

THE OCCASIONAL USE OF THE † TOGETHER WITH A FOOTNOTE (ALSO SEE P. XXXVII)

This marks where a presumed F1 compositorial mistake has led to a meaningless word being set (for example 'speeh' instead of 'speech') and, since there is a 'correct' form of the word offered by either F2–4 or Qq, the correct form of the word rather than the F1 error has been set. The footnote directs the reader to the original F1 setting reproduced at the bottom of the page.

PATTERNED BRACKETS { } SURROUNDING A PREFIX OR PART OF A STAGE DIRECTION

These will be used on the infrequent occasions where a minor alteration or addition has been made to the original F1 setting.

THE VARIED USE OF THE * AND ∞

This will change from text to text. Sometimes (as in *Hamlet*) an * will be used to show where, because of the 1606 Acte To Restraine The Abuses of Players, F1 had to alter Qq's 'God' to 'Heaven'. In other plays it may be used to show the substitution of the archaic 'a' for 'he' while in others the * and /or the ∞ may be used to denote a line from Qq or F2–4 which F1 omits.

THE SYMBOL •

This is a reminder that a character with several prefixes has returned to one previously used in the play.

THE VISUAL SYMBOLS HIGHLIGHTING KEY ITEMS WITHIN THE FIRST FOLIO

THE DROPPING OF THE TEXT A SINGLE LINE

This indicates where one sentence ends, and a new one begins (see pp. xvii–xviii).

THE BOLDING OF PUNCTUATION

This indicates the presence of the major punctuation (see pp. xviii–xxi).

UNBRACKETED STAGE DIRECTIONS

These are the ones presumed to come from the manuscript copy closest to Shakespeare's own hand (F1 sets them centred, on a separate line). They usually have a direct effect on the scene, altering what has been taking place immediately prior to its setting (see p. ix).

BRACKETED STAGE DIRECTIONS

These are the ones presumed to have been added by the Playhouse. (F1 sets them alongside the dialogue, flush to the right of the column.) They usually support, rather than alter, the onstage action (see p. ix).

(The visual difference in the two sets of directions can quickly point the reader to an unexpected aspect of an entry or exit. Occasionally an entry is set alongside the text, rather than on a separate line. This might suggest the character enters not wishing to draw attention to itself, for example, towards the end of *Macbeth,* the servant entering with the dreadful news of the moving Byrnane Wood. Again, F1 occasionally sets an exit on a separate line, perhaps stopping the onstage action altogether, as with the triumphal exit to a 'Gossips feast' at the end of *The Comedy of Errors* made by most of the reunited and/or business pacified characters, leaving the servant Dromio twins onstage to finish off the play. A footnote will be added when these unusual variations in F1's directions occur.)

As with all current texts, the final period of any bracketed or unbracketed stage direction will not be set.

ACT, SCENE, AND LINE NUMBERING SPECIFIC TO THIS TEXT

Each of these scripts will show the act and scene division from F1. They will also indicate modern act and scene division, which often differs from Ff/Qq. Modern texts suggest that in many plays full scene division was not attempted until the eighteenth century, and act division in the early texts was sometimes haphazard at best. Thus many modern texts place the act division at a point other than that set in Ff/Qq, and nearly always break Ff/Qq text up into extra scenes. When modern texts add an act or scene division which is not shared by F1, the addition will be shown in brackets within the body of each individual play as it occurs. When Ff set a new Act or scene, for clarity these texts will start a fresh page, even though this is not Ff/Qq practice

ON THE LEFT HAND SIDE OF EACH PAGE

Down the left of each page, line numbers are shown in increments of five. These refer to the lines in this text only. Where F1 prints a line containing two sentences, since these scripts set two separate lines, each line will be numbered independently.

On The Top Right Of Each Page

These numbers represent the first and last lines set on the page, and so summarise the information set down the left hand side of the text.

At The Bottom Right Of Each Page: using these scripts with other texts

At times a reader may want to compare these texts with either the original First Folio, or a reputable modern text, or both. Specially devised line numbers will make this a fairly easy proposition. These new reference numbers will be found at the bottom right of the page, just above the footnote section.

The information before the colon allows the reader to compare these texts against any photographic reproduction of the First Folio. The information after the colon allows the reader to compare these texts with a modern text, specifically the excellent *Riverside Shakespeare*.[7]

Before the colon: any photostat of the First Folio

A capital letter plus a set of numbers will be shown followed by a lowercase letter. The numbers refer the reader to a particular page within the First Folio; the capital letter before the numbers specifies whether the reader should be looking at the right hand column (R) or left hand column (L) on that particular page; the lower case letter after the numbers indicates which compositor (mainly 'a' through 'e') set that particular column. An occasional asterisk alongside the reference tells the reader that though this is the page number as set in F1, it is in fact numbered out of sequence, and care is needed to ensure, say in *Cymbeline,* the appropriate one of two 'p. 389s' is being consulted.

Since the First Folio was printed in three separate sections (the first containing the Comedies, the second the Histories, and the third the Tragedies),[8] the pages and section in which each of these scripts is to be found will be mentioned in the introduction accompanying each play. The page number refers to that printed at the top of the reproduced Folio page, and not to the number that appears at the bottom of the page of the book which contains the reproduction.

Thus, from this series of texts, page one of *Measure for Measure* shows the ref-

---

[7]   Gwynne Blakemore Evans, Harry Levin, Anne Barton, Herschel Baker, Frank Kermode, Hallet D. Smith, and Marie Edel, eds., *The Riverside Shakespeare* (Copyright © 1974 by Houghton Mifflin Company). This work is chosen for its exemplary scholarship, editing principles, and footnotes.

[8]   The plays known as Romances were not printed as a separate section: *Cymbeline* was set with the Tragedies, *The Winter's Tale* and *The Tempest* were set within the Comedies, and though *Pericles* had been set in Q it did not appear in the compendium until F3. *Troilus and Cressida* was not assigned to any section, but was inserted between the Histories and the Tragedies with only 2 of its 28 pages numbered.

erence 'L61–c'. This tells the reader that the text was set by compositor 'c' and can be checked against the left hand column of p. 61 of the First Folio (*Measure For Measure* being set in the Comedy Section of F1).

Occasionally the first part of the reference seen at the bottom of the page will also be seen within the text, somewhere on the right hand side of the page. This shows the reader exactly where this column has ended and the new one begins.

(As any photostat of the First Folio clearly shows, there are often sixty-five lines or more per column, sometimes crowded very close together. The late Professor Charlton Hinman employed a brilliantly simple line-numbering system (known as TLN, short for Through Line Numbering System) whereby readers could quickly be directed to any particular line within any column on any page.

The current holders of the rights to the TLN withheld permission for the system to be used in conjunction with this series of Folio Texts.)

After the colon: *The Riverside Shakespeare*

Numbers will be printed indicating the act, scene, and line numbers in *The Riverside Shakespeare,* which contain the information set on the particular page of this script. Again, using the first page of *Measure For Measure*, the reference 1.1.1–21 on page one of these scripts directs the reader to Act One Scene 1 of *The Riverside Shakespeare*; line one in *The Riverside Shakespeare* matches the first line in this text, while the last line of dialogue on page one of this text is to be found in line twenty-one of the *Riverside* version of the play.

COMMON TYPESETTING PECULIARITIES
OF THE FOLIO AND QUARTO TEXTS
(And How These Texts Present Them)

There are a few (to modern eyes) unusual contemporary Elizabethan and early Jacobean printing practices which will be retained in these scripts.

THE ABBREVIATIONS, 'S.', 'L.', 'D.', 'M.'

Ff and Qq use standard printing abbreviations when there is not enough space on a single line to fit in all the words. The most recognisable to modern eyes includes 'S.' for Saint; 'L.' for Lord; 'M.' for Mister (though this can also be short for 'Master', 'Monsieur', and on occasions even 'Mistress'); and 'D.' for Duke. These scripts will set F1 and footnote accordingly.

'Ÿ', 'W', AND ACCENTED FINAL VOWELS

Ff/Qq's two most commonly used abbreviations are not current today, viz.:

ÿ, which is usually shorthand for either 'you'; 'thee'; 'thou'; 'thy'; 'thine'; or 'yours'

w, usually with a ¨ above, shorthand for either 'which'; 'what'; 'when'; or 'where'. Also, in other cases of line overcrowding, the last letter of a relatively unimportant word is omitted, and an accent placed over the preceding vowel as a marker, e.g. 'thä' for 'than'. For all such abbreviations these scripts will set F1 and footnote accordingly.

THE SPECIAL CASE OF THE QUESTION AND EXCLAMATION MARKS
('?' AND '!')

USAGE

Elizabethan use of these marks differs somewhat from modern practice. Ff/Qq rarely set an exclamation mark: instead the question mark was used either both as a question mark and as an exclamation point. Thus occasionally the question mark suggests some minor emphasis in the reading.

SENTENCE COUNT

When either mark occurs in the middle of a speech, it can be followed by a capitalised or a lowercase word. When the word is lowercase (not capitalised) the sentence continues on without a break. The opposite is not always true: just because the following word is capitalised does not automatically signify the start of a new sentence, though more often than not it does.

Elizabethan rhetorical writing style allowed for words to be capitalised within a sentence, a practice continued by the F1 compositors. Several times in *The Winters Tale,* highly emotional speeches are set full of question marks followed by capitalised words. Each speech could be either one long sentence of ongoing passionate rush, or up to seven shorter sentences attempting to establish self-control.

The final choice belongs to the individual reader, and in cases where such alternatives arise, the passages will be boxed, footnoted, and the various possibilities discussed.

THE ENDING OF SPEECHES WITH NO PUNCTUATION, OR PUNCTUATION OTHER THAN A PERIOD

Quite often F1–2 will not show punctuation at the end of a speech, or sometimes set a colon (:) or a comma (,) instead. Some commentators suggest the setting of anything other than a period was due to compositor carelessness, and that omission occurred either for the same reason, or because the text was so full it came flush to the right hand side of the column and there was no room left for the final punctuation to be set. Thus modern texts nearly always end a speech with the standard period (.), question mark (?), or exclamation mark (!), no matter what F1–2 have set.

However, omission doesn't always occur when a line is full, and F2, though making over sixteen hundred unauthorised typographical corrections of F1 (more than eight hundred of which are accepted by most modern texts), rarely replaces an offending comma or colon with a period, or adds missing periods—F3 is the first to make such alterations on a large scale basis. A few commentators, while acknowledging some of the omissions/mistakes are likely to be due to compositor or scribal error, suggest that ending the speech with anything other than a period (or not ending the speech at all) might indicate that the character with the speech immediately following is in fact interrupting this first speaker.

These texts will set F1, footnote accordingly, and sometimes discuss the possible effect of the missing or 'incorrect' punctuation.

THE SUBSTITUTIONS OF 'i/I' FOR 'j/J' AND 'u' FOR 'v'

In both Ff/Qq words now spelled as 'Jove' or 'Joan' are often set as 'Iove' or 'Ioan'. To avoid confusion, these texts will set the modern version of the word. Similarly, words with 'v' in the middle are often set by Ff/Qq with a 'u'; thus the modern word 'avoid' becomes 'auoid'. Again, these texts will set the modern version of the word, without footnote acknowledgement.

ALTERNATIVE SETTINGS OF A WORD WHERE DIFFERENT SPELLINGS MAINTAIN THE SAME MEANING

Ff/Qq occasionally set, what appears to modern eyes, an archaic spelling of a word for which there is a more common modern alternative, for example 'murther' for murder, 'burthen' for burden, 'moe' for more, 'vilde' for vile. Some modern texts set the Ff/Qq spelling, some modernise. These texts will set the F1 spelling throughout.

ALTERNATIVE SETTINGS OF A WORD WHERE DIFFERENT SPELLINGS SUGGEST DIFFERENT MEANINGS

Far more complicated is the situation where, while an Elizabethan could substitute one word formation for another and still imply the same thing, to modern eyes the substituted word has a entirely different meaning to the one it has replaced. The following is by no means an exclusive list of the more common dual-spelling, dual-meaning words:

anticke–antique	mad–made	sprite–spirit
born–borne	metal–mettle	sun–sonne
hart–heart	mote–moth	travel–travaill
human–humane	pour–(powre)–power	through–thorough
lest–least	reverent–reverend	troth–truth
lose–loose	right–rite	whether–whither

Some of these doubles offer a metrical problem too; for example 'sprite', a one syllable word, versus 'spirit'. A potential problem occurs in *A Midsummer Nights Dream*, where provided the modern texts set Q1's 'thorough', the scansion pattern of elegant magic can be established, whereas F1's more plebeian 'through' sets up a much more awkward and clumsy moment.

These texts will set the F1 reading, and footnote where the modern texts' substitution of a different word formation has the potential to alter the meaning (and sometimes scansion) of the line.

'THEN' AND 'THAN'

These two words, though their neutral vowels sound different to modern ears, were almost identical to Elizabethan speakers and readers, despite their different meanings. Ff and Qq make little distinction between them, setting them interchangeably. In these scripts the original printings will be used, and the modern reader should soon get used to substituting one for the other as necessary.

'I', AND 'AY'

Ff/Qq often print the personal pronoun 'I' and the word of agreement 'aye' simply as 'I'. Again, the modern reader should quickly get used to this and make the substitution whenever necessary. The reader should also be aware that very occasionally either word could be used and the phrase make perfect sense, even though different meanings would be implied.

'MY SELFE/HIM SELFE/HER SELFE' VERSUS 'MYSELF/HIMSELF/ HERSELF'

Generally Ff/Qq separate the two parts of the word, 'my selfe' while most modern texts set the single word 'myself'. The difference is vital, based on Elizabethan philosophy. Elizabethans regarded themselves as composed of two parts, the corporeal 'I', and the more spiritual part, the 'selfe'. Thus when an Elizabethan character refers to 'my selfe', he or she is often referring to what is to all intents and purposes a separate being, even if that being is a particular part of him- or herself. Thus soliloquies can be thought of as a debate between the 'I' and 'my selfe', and in such speeches, even though there may be only one character onstage, it's as if there were two distinct entities present.

These texts will show F1 as set.

FOOTNOTE CODE
(shown in two forms, the first alphabetical, the second grouping the codes by topic)

To help the reader focus on a particular topic or research aspect, a special code has been developed for these texts. Each footnote within the footnote section at the bottom of each page of text has a single letter or series of letters placed in front of it guiding readers to one specific topic; thus 'SPD' will direct readers to footnotes just dealing with songs, poems, and doggerel.

ALPHABETICAL FOOTNOTE CODING

A	asides
AB	abbreviation
ADD	a passage modern texts have added to their texts from F2–4 / Qq
ALT	a passage (including act and scene division) that has been altered by modern texts without any Ff / Qq authority
COMP	a setting probably influenced by compositor interference
F	concerning disputed facts within the play
FL	foreign language
L	letter or letters
LS	alterations in line structure
M	Shakespeare's use of the scansion of magic (trochaic and seven syllables)
N	a name modern texts have changed or corrected for easier recognition
O	F1 words or phrases substituted for a Qq oath or blasphemy
OM	passage, line, or word modern texts omit or suggest omitting
P	change in prefix assigned to a character
PCT	alterations to F1's punctuation by modern and/or contemporary texts
Q	material rejected or markedly altered by Qq not usually set by modern texts
QO	oaths or blasphemies set in Qq not usually set by modern texts
SD	stage directions added or altered by modern texts
SP	a solo split line for a single character (see pp. xv–xvi above)

SPD	matters concerning songs, poems, or doggerel
?ST	where, because of question marks within the passage, the final choice as to the number of sentences is left to the reader's discretion
STRUCT	a deliberate change from the F1 setting by these texts
UE	an unusual entrance (set to the side of the text) or exit (set on a separate line)
VP	F1's verse altered to prose or vice versa, or lines indistinguishable as either
W	F1's word or phrase altered by modern texts
WHO	(in a convoluted passage) who is speaking to whom
WS	F1 line structure altered because of casting off problems (see pp. x–xi above)

FOOTNOTE CODING BY TOPIC

STAGE DIRECTIONS, ETC.

A	asides
P	change in prefix assigned to a character
SD	stage directions added or altered by modern texts
UE	an unusual entrance (set to the side of the text) or exit (set on a separate line)
WHO	(in a convoluted passage) who is speaking to whom

LINE STRUCTURE AND PUNCTUATION, ETC.

L	letter or letters
LS	alterations in line structure
M	Shakespeare's use of the scansion of magic (trochaic and seven syllables)
PCT	alterations to F1's punctuation by modern and/or contemporary texts
SPD	matters concerning songs, poems, or doggerel
?ST	where, because of question marks within the passage, the final choice as to the number of sentences is left to the reader's discretion
SP	a solo split line for a single character (see pp. xv–xvi above)
VP	F1's verse altered to prose or vice versa, or lines indistinguishable as either

WS	F1 line structure altered because of casting off problems (see pp. x–xi above)

CHANGES TO WORDS AND PHRASES

AB	abbreviation
F	concerning disputed facts within the play
FL	foreign language
N	a name modern texts have changed or corrected for easier recognition
O	F1 words or phrases substituted for a Qq oath or blasphemy
QO	oaths or blasphemies set in Qq not usually set by modern texts
W	F1's word or phrase altered by modern texts

CHANGES ON A LARGER SCALE AND OTHER UNAUTHORISED CHANGES

ADD	a passage modern texts have added to their texts from F2–4/Qq
ALT	a passage (including act and scene division) that has been altered by modern texts without any Ff/Qq authority
COMP	a setting probably influenced by compositor interference
OM	passage, line, or word modern texts omit or suggest omitting
Q	material rejected or markedly altered by Qq not usually set by modern texts
STRUCT	a deliberate change from the F1 setting by these texts

ONE MODERN CHANGE FREQUENTLY NOTED IN THESE TEXTS

'MINUTE' CHANGES TO THE SYLLABLE LENGTH OF FF LINES

As noted above on pages xi–xii, modern texts frequently correct what commentators consider to be large scale metric deficiencies, often to the detriment of character and scene. There are many smaller changes made too, especially when lines are either longer or shorter than the norm of pentameter by 'only' one or two syllables. These changes are equally troublesome, for there is a highly practical theatrical rule of thumb guideline to such irregularities, viz.:

if lines are slightly **longer** than pentameter, then the characters so involved have too much information coursing through them to be contained within the 'norms' of proper verse, occasionally even to the point of losing self-control

if lines are slightly **shorter** than ten syllables, then either the information therein contained or the surrounding action is creating a momentary (almost need to breath) hesitation, sometimes suggesting a struggle to maintain self-control

These texts will note all such alterations, usually offering the different syllable counts per line as set both by F1 and by the altered modern texts, often with a brief suggestion as to how the original structural 'irregularity' might reflect onstage action.

FINALLY, A BRIEF WORD ABOUT THE COMPOSITORS [9]

Concentrated research into the number of the compositors and their habits began in the 1950s and, for a while, it was thought five men set the First Folio, each assigned a letter, 'A' through 'E'.

'E' was known to be a seventeen-year-old apprentice whose occasional mishaps both in copying text and securing the type to the frame have led to more than a few dreadful lapses, notably in *Romeo and Juliet*, low in the left column on p. 76 of the Tragedies, where in sixteen F1 lines he commits seven purely typographical mistakes. Compositor 'B' set approximately half of F1, and has been accused of being cavalier both with copying text and not setting line ending punctuation when the line is flush to the column edge. He has also been accused of setting most of the so called 'solo' split lines, though a comparison of other compositors' habits suggests they did so too, especially the conglomerate once considered to be the work of a single compositor known as 'A'. It is now acknowledged that the work set by 'A' is probably the work of at least two and more likely five different men, bringing the total number of compositors having worked on F1 to nine ('A' times five, and 'B' through 'E').

It's important to recognise that the work of these men was sometimes flawed. Thus the footnotes in these texts will point the reader to as many examples as possible which current scholarship and research suggest are in error. These errors fall into two basic categories. The first is indisputable, that of pure typographical mistakes ('wh?ch' for 'which'): the second, frequently open to challenge, is failure to copy exactly the text (Qq or manuscript) which F1 has used as its source material.

As for the first, these texts place the symbol † before a footnote marker within the text (not in the footnote section), a combination used only to point to a purely typographical mistake. Thus in the error-riddled section of *Romeo and Juliet* quoted above, p. 109 of this script shows fourteen footnote markers, seven of them coupled with the symbol †. Singling out these typographical-only markers alerts the reader to compositor error, and that (usually) the 'correct' word or phrase has been set within the text. Thus the reader doesn't have to bother with the footnote below unless they have a morbid curiosity to find out what the error actually is. Also, by definition, the more † appearing in a passage, the worse set that passage is.

As to the second series of (sometimes challengeable) errors labelled poor copy work, the footnotes will alert the reader to the alternative Qq word or phrase usage preferred by most modern texts, often discussing the alternatives in detail, especially when there seems to be validity to the F1 setting.

---

[9] Readers are directed to the ground breaking work of Alice Walker, and also to the ongoing researches of Paul Werstine and Peter W. M. Blayney.

Given the fluid state of current research, more discoveries are bound to be published as to which compositor set which F1 column long after these texts go to print. Thus the current assignation of compositors at the bottom of each of these scripts' pages represents what is known at this moment, and will be open to reassessment as time goes by.

A CAVEAT: THE COMPOSITORS AND 'SINGLE SPLIT LINES' (SEE PP. XV–XVI)

Many commentators suggest single split lines are not Shakespearean dramatic necessity, but compositorial invention to get out of a typesetting dilemma. Their argument is threefold:

first, as mentioned on pp. x–xi, because of 'white space' a small amount of text would have to be artificially expanded to fill a large volume of what would otherwise be empty space: therefore, even though the column width could easily accommodate regular verse lines, the line or lines would be split in two to fill an otherwise embarrassing gap

second, even though the source documents the compositors were using to set F1 showed material as a single line of verse, occasionally there was too much text for the F1 column to contain it as that one single line: hence the line had to be split in two

third, the device was essentially used by compositor B.

There is no doubt that sometimes single split lines did occur for typesetting reasons, but it should be noted that:

single split lines are frequently set well away from white space problems

often the 'too-much-text-for-the-F1-column-width' problem is solved by setting the last one or two words of the overly lengthy line either as a new line, or as an overflow or underflow just above the end of the existing line without resorting to the single split line

all compositors seem to employ the device, especially the conglomerate known as 'A' and compositor E.

As regards the following text, while at times readers will be alerted to the fact that typographical problems could have had an influence on the F1 setting, when single split lines occur their dramatic potential will be discussed, and readers are invited to explore and accept or reject the setting accordingly.

INTRODUCTION TO THE TEXT OF
THE TRAGEDIE OF CYMBELINE, KING OF BRITAINE[1]
pages 369–993, the latter incorrectly numbered, of the Tragedy Section of the First Folio[2]

All Act, Scene, and line numbers will refer to the
Applause text below unless otherwise stated.

Considered one of the four Romances (the others being *Pericles, The Winters Tale,* and *The Tempest*), there has been much speculation as to the provenance and dating of this play. Its first recorded performance was during late April 1611 at The Globe, as noted by the astrologer and necromancer Simon Forman. Critics have suggested the play was written as early as 1604 or 1605, though contemporary research suggests the later dates of somewhere between 1608–1610. Some scholars suggest it followed *The Winters Tale,* others that it preceded it, thus its probable order in the canon is either as play #34 or #35.

Doubts have been expressed as to whether Shakespeare wrote the complete play. One theory is that he only wrote the first two Acts, and then revised what interested him, which in some eyes explains the complete disappearance of Posthumus until he is hastily (and clumsily, so such critics argue) brought back into the play at the beginning of Act Five. Another suggestion is that he wrote the Imogen scenes and the love story connected with it and then, in collaboration, supervised the scenes involving Cymbeline, Belarius, and the Masque.

Neither theory seems widely supported now, though many doubts still exist as to the authenticity of the Masque, Act Five Scene 4, pp. 117–9 this script. Several scholars suggest that it is so clumsy that it could only be the work of an unspecified 'co-worker', arguing a possibly similar intrusion to that of the Wedding Masque of Act Four of *The Tempest.*

The text was not seen in print until the First Folio (F1) publication of 1623 which is thus the only authoritative source text. Initially there was some disagreement as to whether the text was set by just one compositor, B, or whether he had help from the accident-prone apprentice E. It is now believed E probably set five of the play's thirty-one pages.

There is no doubt that the material was prepared by the scrivener Ralph Crane

---

[1]   For a detailed examination, see Stanley Wells and Gary Taylor, eds., *William Shakespeare: A Textual Companion* (Oxford: Clarendon Press, 1987), pp. 604–11; for a detailed analysis of the play's contents, see any of the Recommended Modern Texts.

[2]   *Mr. William Shakespeare's Comedies, Histories, & Tragedies,* 1623.

but not from a prompt copy. Though not of the theatre (his principle work was to copy material for lawyers), Crane was involved in the preparation of at least five plays for the Folio as well as two plays for Thomas Middleton. Scholars characterise his work as demonstrating regular and careful scene and act division; dramatis personae and sometimes locale noted at the end of the text (space permitting); careful and heavy use of punctuation; frequent use of parentheses, apostrophes, and hyphens; massed entry techniques (where all characters with entries into the scene are listed in a single direction at the top of the scene irrespective of where in the action they are supposed to enter); few stage directions, often expressed in a more literary manner than displayed in playhouse or authorial directions. There is also the consensus that Crane's work appears clear and accurate.

Excellent research has offered suggestions as to the conjectured origins of the script from which Crane and thus the Folio developed their texts. It seems there were two copyists involved for, as noted in the Oxford *Textual Companion* (op. cit.), there are a (limited) number of spelling changes from Act Two Scene Five onwards which differ from the first part of the text and which are not characteristic of the compositors who set the text nor, presumably, to Crane himself. Though the text is probably too long to come from a copy readied for performance, the stage directions move from practical notation at the play's opening to a much more long-winded literary style (one of Crane's known practices) by the start of Act Five. To further reinforce the literary rather than playhouse quality of the text, no music cues are offered before the battles (as would be customary in a script annotated by the playhouse) and virtually no properties are listed.

As with *The Winters Tale,* commentators suggest whatever Crane based his copy upon was very sound. In his excellent introduction, J.M. Nosworthy, editor of *The Arden Shakespeare Cymbeline,*[3] comments that the final composition of the Folio text reveals 'neatness and symmetry... [with]... a total of some sixty errors, yielding the comparatively satisfactory average of two per page'.

Despite such reassurances, the Oxford *Textual Companion*[4] lists some fifty F1 passages involving eighty or so lines that an editor would need to restructure to create a modern edition of the play, not including any revision of the Masque. Some of these proposals, though seemingly minor, are quite disconcerting. Consequently, there are a few textual problems arising from an examination of F1.

IMOGEN OR INNOGEN?

The name of Imogen will be kept as is, though the Oxford *Textual Companion* (op. cit.) argues strenuously for 'Innogen'. It suggests both the source material from

---

[3]   J. M. Nosworthy, ed., *Cymbeline—The Arden Shakespeare* (London: Methuen & Co. Ltd., 1962.)

[4]   op. cit. as #1 above, pp. 663

Holinshed and the diary commentary by Simon Forman use the form 'Innogen', adding that the name 'Imogen' is not to be found in the English language until after publication of the play. It conjectures that the corruption of 'Innogen' to 'Imogen' occurred because either the scribes or the printers mistook the penmanship on the 'nn' for a single 'm' — what is known technically as a 'minim error'.

THE MASQUE

This has been the subject of much intense questioning.

The Ff text is very erratic, with the supposedly alternating 8/6 syllable lines being broken by occasional 4 syllable and 14 syllable lines. Most modern texts smooth out these breaks, often concluding that the masque is non-Shakespearean. However, Wilson Knight, Hardin Craig, and J. M. Nosworthy (among others) convincingly argue that the passage is essentially Shakespearean, and this text can do no better than re-quote Hardin Craig as already cited in Professor Nosworthy's exemplary introduction to his Arden edition of the play (op. cit.):

> All in all, it seems possible to defend the authenticity of the masque and other stylistic abnormalities on the ground that gods and those who speak to gods, especially
> if they themselves are spirits, must speak differently from creatures of this world.
> Hardin Craig, 'Shakespeare's Bad Poetry', *Shakespeare Survey*, 1, p. 55.

Nosworthy goes on to argue that the section is essentially written in the '14-er' rhyme pattern of the 1590s, and reproduces the first speech of the Masque accordingly.[5] Unfortunately he does not print the complete Masque in the main body of his text that way. This is an excellent argument and, when the text is set thus to paper it is easy to see the predominant pattern of doublets and triplets which are occasionally broken by shorter lines at the more stressful or ritual moments.

If the Masque is to be sung, or spoken ritually, then the layout of the modern texts, or Nosworthy's amendment as shown in the body of this text, offers the smoothest transitions, with the latter still allowing scope for character variation within the piece. If the text is to be explored psychologically, acted perhaps as an extension of Posthumus' restlessness, then the original F1 layout has a lot to offer, with the Mother's short lines suggesting it is difficult for her to continue, while the very long lines spoken later by the men suggest their increasing passion.

This edition will take the unusual step of not following F1's layout, setting instead the dialogue on the principle of the Nosworthy argument. The F1 setting will be printed as an Appendix. Actors and readers are invited to explore and choose between the F1 layout as shown there, the Nosworthy amendment, and the modern poetical restructurings — the latter two to be found and occasionally annotated in the main body of the text, pp. 117–118.

---

[5]   op. cit. page xxxv

A PREFIX CONFUSION

Cymbeline's two young sons were stolen as infants by Morgan, a then unjustly out-of-favour commander. Morgan is known throughout the play, both in name and prefix, by his alias, Belarius. However, the prefixes assigned the two princes are their original princely names, Guiderius and Arviragus, a clue as to how the characters might be played perhaps. Unfortunately for the reader, in their onstage lives they have never been called by these names, but by their aliases. Thus, whenever they are referred to by Belarius and Imogen, or by each other, Guiderius' onstage name is Philidore, and Arviragus is known as Cadwall.

THREE CONFUSING FACTS

There seem to be **several different women attending Imogen.** As she prepares for bed, Imogen asks for 'my woman Helene' who briefly enters (2.2.2, p. 35). The following morning, when she finds her bracelet missing—the one Iachimo stole—she bids Pisanio go to 'Dorothy my woman' to see if she has found it. Dorothy appears to be a 'ghost' character, one with neither onstage action nor text, for she is never named again, thus the naming of two women as Imogen's attendants may be a matter of confusion on Shakespeare's part. As it stands there could be just one 'woman' or two, or, as will be seen in a moment, even more.

Whatever the decision there will be a minor complication. Cloten, the Queene's son, insists on wooing Imogen despite repeated offstage repulses. He knocks at Imogen's chamber early on the morning after the theft of the bracelet, and is answered by an unnamed 'Lady' who from the dialogue is yet another who serves Imogen. She is never referred to by name. Is this Helene, the ghost Dorothy, or another character? The possibility of another character exists, for there are an unspecified number of unnamed Ladies attending the Queene's early morning herb-gathering (p. 19). With so many subtle traces of the Queene's treachery throughout the play, might one of Imogen's (one, two, or three) women actually be the Queene's spy?

As usual with a literary rather than a Playhouse script providing the manuscript copy for the F1 setting of the play, there are occasionally **an unspecified number of smaller characters** such as the (by no means exclusive) following examples; the Roman Tribunes talking to the two Senators (p. 84, Act Three Scene 8); the Ladies accompanying the Queene (p. 19, Act One Scene 6); the Lords attending Cymbeline throughout; the Attendants (whether English or Roman) in the declaration of war sequence (p. 53, Act Three Scene 1); the Roman Prisoners (p. 125) in Act Five Scene 5. How few, or how many, is up to each reader's imagination.

Finally, **who sings the song on p. 39, and how?** This question surrounds Cloten's early morning wooing of Imogen, for which occasion he has gathered an unspecified number of onstage Musitians. It could be appallingly sung by Cloten, it could be beautifully sung by a specially hired professional singer. The answer may be tipped in beauty's favour, for as one of the Romances, the play was originally intended to delight the audience with pageantry and music as well as plot and poetry.

THE SUMMARIES

Occasionally concise little summaries of the action suddenly appear, delivered as direct addresses by a single character to the audience. Critics often wonder if these are Shakespearean, since they do not show the usual characteristic of a Shakespearean soliloquy in that

> they do little to reveal the state of the character's mind, or provide the character with any new answers to problems with which they may be faced

> they basically summarise what has occurred or add new information, often ending with a fervent prayer for events to improve

They are set at frequent intervals after Act One finishes, disappearing before Act Five's special spectacle, the Masque on pp. 117–119. As written, the summaries could well be for those audience members who arrived late or were inattentive to the somewhat convoluted plot.

These sometimes clumsy speeches are spoken by the 2nd. Lord, Act Two Scene 1, p. 34; Belarius, Act Three Scene 3, pp. 62–63; the Queene, pp. 74–75, Cloten, pp. 77–78, and Pisanio, p. 78, all short sequences towards the end of Act Three Scene 5; and Pisanio, Act Four Scene 3, p. 104.

STANDARD MODERN TEXT TIDYING OF THE FIRST FOLIO

METRICAL TIDYING

There are few line structure changes, but when they occur they seem important, especially in the last scene, and readers are encouraged to decide whether Ff's untidiness denotes an irregular moment for the character, or is simply a mistake. A tiny example will suffice.

In the angry interchange between Cymbeline and Imogen over her marrying Posthumus instead of Cloten, Ff set a series of slightly irregular lines. Father and daughter are in the midst of comparing the virtues of the man each prefers, each in their own biased way; the numbers in brackets refer to the syllable count in each line:

Imogen	O blessed, that I might not: I chose an Eagle;	(12)
	And did avoyd a Puttocke.	(7)
Cymbeline	Thou took'st a Begger, would'st have made my	(9)
	Throne, a Seate for basenesse.	(6)
Imogen	No, I rather added a lustre to it.	(11)

Cymbeline	O thou vilde one!	(4)
Imogen	Sir,	(1)
	It is your fault that I have lov'd Posthumus:	(11)

(p. 7, ll. 1.2.96–103)

Following the opening long line, the gaps implied by Ff's series of short lines suggest one of two totally different readings.

If the short lines are used as hesitations, each character would be doing their very best to try to stay in control, perhaps holding back their anger . The underlying subtext might well be one of a father and daughter who very much love each other and are doing everything possible not to damage the relationship any further. The only ensuing long (eleven syllable) line belongs to Imogen's assertion that the choice she has made will reflect well on the Crown, not damage it as Cymbeline suggests.

If the short lines are used as overlapping lines, as some critics suggest, the sequence quickly degenerates into a dreadful family row where neither person is listening.

Either way, the Ff setting suggest something out of the ordinary is taking place. Not so most modern texts. With so many irregular lines, especially short ones, most editors reconstruct the passage as follows

Imogen	O blessed, that I might not: I chose an Eagle;	(12)
	And did avoyd a Puttocke.	(7)
Cymbeline	Thou took'st a Begger, would'st have made my Throne	(10)
	A Seate for basenesse.	
Imogen	No, I rather added	(10)
	A lustre to it.	
Cymbeline	O thou vilde one!	
Imogen	Sir,	(10)
	It is your fault that I have lov'd Posthumus:	(11)

Ff's eight lines have been reduced to six: the only short line that remains provides a moment's hesitation for Cymbeline. Metrically, the final four lines of the sequence are basic pentameter, implying each character is in full control, and is quick to contradict as soon as the other person finishes. Ff's potential of either attempted control or the screaming match has essentially been replaced by speed of debate.

This is not a matter of right or wrong: simply, there are differences. While the angry content has not been altered, the way of expressing it most certainly has. And readers are invited to judge for themselves which setting, Ff or modern, appeals to them under the circumstances.

In this, and all similarly altered passages, this text will set F1 as is, and the alterations will be footnoted and discussed in some detail.

CHANGES IN PUNCTUATION

Despite Crane's acknowledged care, some alterations are inevitable. For example, understandable yet probably theatrically damaging punctuation changes are found as Iachimo closely inspects Imogen's bedroom and her body.

Once out of the trunk he is immediately drawn to her as she sleeps. He has already called her Venus (the reference to Cytherea) as he praised her beauty, said how much he wants to touch her, repeated twice that he wants to kiss her. His attention focuses on her lips, then the sweetness of her breath, and finally her eyes, from all of which he eventually forces himself away.

Starting with his lip fixation, F1 sets part of the speech as follows, with the asterisks marking two periods modern texts have difficulty in accepting

> Rubies unparagon'd,
> How deerely they do it: 'Tis her breathing that
> Perfumes the Chamber thus: the Flame o'th'Taper
> Bowes toward her, and would under-peepe her lids. *
>
> To see th'inclosed Lights, now Canopied
> Under these windowes, White and Azure lac'd
> With Blew of Heavens owne tinct.
> But my designe. *
> To note the Chamber, I will write all downe
> (p. 36, ll. 2.2.23–31)

Logically, grammatically, most modern texts set the first asterisked moment as

> the Flame o'th'Taper
> Bowes toward her, and would under-peepe her lids, *
> To see th'inclosed Lights, now Canopied
> Under these windowes, White and Azure lac'd
> With Blew of Heavens owne tinct.

That is, it is the flame which wants to see the blue of Imogen's eyes, a fine poetic conceit.

But poetry may not be uppermost in Iachimo's mind at this moment, for the speech to date shows him to be highly aroused and, as the speech continues, though wanting to pin down details of the room and attempting to do so, his gaze keeps returning to Imogen's body. The first ungrammatical Ff period shown above makes it abundantly clear that while the Flame o'th Taper would like to see her eyes, so would he. The F1 start to the new sentence, 'To see th'inclosed lights', suggests a fervent almost prayer-like plea for himself to be allowed to gaze into her eyes right now.

Similarly, most modern texts remove the second period, thus:

> But my designe *
> To note the Chamber: I will write all downe

Again, this is both correct grammar (supplying a verb to a sentence that other-wise wouldn't have one) and fine logic. But Ff's second ungrammatical period sug-gests a man desperately reminding himself as firmly and as quickly as possible to get away from her body before he does something stupid, and to get on with amassing details whereby he can win his bet. F1's 'But my design.' has all the desperation an actor would ever need to make his point; the modern texts' repunctuation reduces Iachimo's action from desperation to almost a matter of practicality.

This text will set Ff's punctuation as is, and will only footnote and comment on the modern texts' repunctuation if a change in matters theatrical might occur as a result.

THE SHARED OR SPLIT LINES OF VERSE

As discussed in pp. v–viii in the General Introduction, these are lines shared by two characters which speed up the pace at which a second character springboards off the words of a first. This is used to great effect in the interchanges between Imogen and Iachimo when left alone by Pisanio, as she seeks to find news of Posthumus and he a way to seduce her, pp. 25–8. With their repeated quick re-sponses to each other it is almost as if both characters are afraid of silence.

THE SINGLE SPLIT-LINE

These are found infrequently in the this text, but when they are, there may be tiny clues in the exchange. The principles are discussed on p. xv-xvi of the General Introduction and here are two quick examples.

Though the modern texts set as one line Pisanio's meaningless reassurance for Imogen that she shall see her banished husband soon

> Be assur'd Madam, with his next vantage.

Ff allow him a little more care while answering, setting the reply as two short lines, thus:

> Be assur'd Madam,   (5)
> With the next vantage.   (5)
> (p. 12, ll. 1.4.29–30)

Similarly, the Lady from the Queene makes a standard single line entry to give Imogen a message

> The Queene (Madam) desires your Highnesse Company.

a normal metric setting. However, the Ff settings show a woman much more aware that she is intruding on something private, and perhaps worthy of reporting back to her Mistress,

> The Queene (Madam)   (4)
> Desires your Highnesse Company   (8)
>   (p. 12, ll. 1.4.45–46)

While in each case the modern resetting is correct in terms of verse, the Ff single split lines offer each of the characters a moment somewhat more complex and more important than the standardised metrics convey.

In the case of both sets of split lines, this text will set Ff as is, and draw the reader's attention to these moments with the appropriate symbol (the decorative bracket '}' for the shared line, the '→' for the solo split line) and footnote where necessary.

VERSE AND PROSE

There are very few examples of Ff's verse or prose being restructured. The major examples are when the two Lords are with Cloten, where there is the possibility of much of the 2nd. Lord's virulent anti-Cloten asides being in verse, though the modern texts set prose throughout. Certainly when finally alone with the audience this 2nd. Lord uses nothing but verse to express his dislike for Cloten's mother, the Queene, and to wish Imogen well. Expressing the dislike-of-Cloten-asides in verse would also show a delicacy and control which separates in style as well as content the 2nd. Lord from the 1st. Lord and Cloten who mainly use prose in their scenes together. (For fuller details see footnotes #1 on p. 9 and #1 on p. 32.)

STAGE DIRECTIONS

As with most F1 texts set from literary manuscripts, this play is fairly complete with significant entries, exits, and major incidents that stop or become the onstage action. As usual the stage directions lack many of the details that can be quickly gleaned from following the dialogue or action of the play, such as minor exits and (re-)entries of secondary characters, the passing of letters, the gathering of properties, and asides.

DIRECTIONS WHICH COULD BE GATHERED FROM THE DIALOGUE

Since the manuscripts and texts upon which the Qq/Ff are based were originally prepared for the theatre, it would be second nature for the actors and prompt book holder to fill in many of the smaller details without extra annotation. Thus these minor details would not make their way to the various publishing houses, and it was never considered a necessity by the publishers to add such missing details, since, as often as not, they weren't really missing if the text in question was closely followed.

While modern texts feel it necessary to add a stage direction for Posthumus' handing over his ring to seal his bet with Iachimo, the Elizabethans using the script wouldn't need it, since Posthumus' line 'heere's my Ring' (p. 17 1.5.160–1) says it all. (The question of to whom he gives it for safekeeping is up to the reader, a minor though important decision, since in Act Two Scene 4 Posthumus seems to hand it directly to Iachimo, with 'Heere, take this too' 2.4.143, p. 49.) Similarly Iachimo's offer to shake hands and Posthumus' acceptance seems to be covered in Iachimo's two brief phrases 'Your hand, a Covenent:', p. 18, l. 1.5.179.

Information can be given before or as the event occurs, for example Iachimo's handing over of Imogen's letters to Posthumus is covered in Iachimo's line 'Heere are Letters for you', p. 46, l. 2.4.45.

Sometimes properties are explained in detail some time after they have been used, for example Imogen's withdrawing something from her bosom that would keep Pisanio's sword from hitting her heart, heralded in the lines

> Come, heere's my heart:
> Something's a-foot: Soft, soft, wee'l no defence,
> Obedient as the Scabbard.
>
> (p. 66, ll. 3.4.108–110)

the 'something' being revealed moments later as earlier love letters from her husband,

> The Scriptures of the Loyall Leonatus
> All turn'd to heresie?
>
> (p. 67, ll. 2.4.112–113)

In these and similar cases, the modern texts offer additional stage directions. In many such cases this text will not, but it will footnote the more difficult and obscure references which need additional direction and/or explanation. Nevertheless, nearly 100 of the 370-plus footnotes offered in this text deal with either stage directions (coded SD), asides (coded A), or with who is speaking to whom (coded WHO).

ASIDES, AND WHO TO WHOM?

Asides are lines usually spoken by a character on the fringes of the scene, and intended just for self-expression or to be heard only by those on the edge of the scene with them. Much of the 2nd. Lord's utter contempt for Cloten is expressed this way, notably in Act One Scene 3, pp. 9 and 10, and in Act Two Scene 1, pp. 32–3.

Often an aside is fairly obvious from the action of the play, for if some or all of the other characters heard it, all hell would break loose, as would be the case with the 2nd. Lord above, or for the doctor, Cornelius. He confides to the audience that both his dislike and distrust of the Queene are reasons for giving her a sleeping draught instead of the poison she has asked for, pp. 20–21, ll. 1.6.48–62.

But it is not always certain that what modern texts mark as asides are necessarily asides.

Some texts suggest that, following his banishment, Posthumus' blessing

> The Gods protect you,

> And blesse the good Remainders of the Court:
> I am gone.
>
> (p. 6, 1.2.79–81)

is an aside intended just for his beloved Imogen. This may be so, but it could also be addressed directly to Cymbeline, despite the angry confrontation. If to Cymbeline it would show a noblesse and forgiveness which would make Posthumus well worthy of his final reconciliation with Imogen, despite his ensuing stupidity. If the remarks are made just to Imogen as an aside, the moment, though understandable, could mark him as somewhat petulant. In view of his later (as he admits by Act Five, misguided) attempts to have Imogen killed on circumstantial evidence of adultery, he needs all the early help he can get to remind the audience of his worthiness.

As with asides, sometimes it is already fairly obvious from the text, when the modern texts suggest that part of a speech is being addressed to a particular character, as in the case of Iachimo's request

> Beseech you Sir,
> Desire my Mans abode, where I did leave him:
> He's strange and peevish.
>
> (p. 25, ll. 1.7.66–68)

Since, apart from Iachimo, Pisanio is the only other male in the scene, the lines have to be delivered to him. Nevertheless, since the lines appear in a speech so far addressed only to Imogen, most modern texts add a stage direction explaining to the reader who these lines are for.

Sometimes this is a useful reminder, but sometimes such a single-minded decision can do harm to a scene. For example, late in the play the audience is told that the Queene has been steadily poisoning Cymbeline since their recent (his second) marriage, so as to get control of the Crown and country. This further explains her eagerness to marry off her biological son Cloten to the King's daughter Imogen, who is only her daughter by marriage.

The first scene of the play explains in detail that Cymbeline is furious with his once-beloved daughter for marrying the child he has reared from infancy, the once thought worthy Posthumus Leonatus. The audience's first sight of Cymbeline shows a very angry man, publicly blasting his daughter, while not listening to her very well reasoned, though equally hot-headed, replies (perhaps the poison has already begun its work).

At the height of the argument, as the Queene reenters, Cymbeline is given the lines

> Thou foolish thing;
> They were againe together: you have done
> Not after our command. Away with her,

> And pen her up.
>
> (p. 7, ll. 1.2.111–115)

There is little doubt that 'They were againe together' is directed towards the Queene, and that 'Away with her, and pen her up' is to some of the unspecified number of Lords attending him, as most modern texts direct.

There is less certainty over 'you have done/Not after our command'. Is this a continuation to the Queene, as some modern texts would have it, or is it to Imogen? Either is possible, though the extra 'to and fro' quality of directing it to Imogen would add a certain frenetic and irrational quality to both character and scene.

But the biggest question concerns the opening phrase, 'Thou foolish thing'. Most modern texts are polite enough to keep the insult as part of the previous public put-downs of Imogen. But it could equally, and more testily, be directed towards the Queene as she reenters. Since Ff set no guide, readers are free to make their own choice. Most modern texts have done it for them, usually without listing the alternatives. Not only is the full potential of the scene thereby restricted, the very starting point for, and further development of, Cymbeline (one of the important characters within the play despite being onstage for a very small proportion of the time), has been predetermined, possibly incorrectly.

Most of what the modern texts consider to be asides or 'who to's?' will be footnoted in this text, with the more dubious open to further discussion in the footnote section at the bottom of each page.

ACTIONS WHICH MAY NEED EXPLANATION

Even though generally evident from the dialogue, some actions need elaboration.

Sometimes exits are too unspecified, such as the generalised Ff 'Exit' or 'Exeunt' not mentioning either who leaves or (via the usual notation 'manet') who remains.

Often exits for the smaller characters are left unmarked. Occasionally this can be awkward, as with the Musitians whom Cloten commands 'get you gone', (p. 39, l. 2.3.28) but are not given a specific direction as to when they leave. Presumably they must exit without too much fuss (so as not upstage Cloten's soliloquy) before the entry of Cymbeline and the Queene in three-and-a-half lines' time, but Ff never precisely indicate where.

Sometimes there are so many details about the properties to be involved in the scene, a timely reminder is well worth while. Such is the case with all the paraphernalia surrounding Iachimo's stealing of the bracelet from the sleeping Imogen's arm, Act Two Scene 2, pp. 35–7. Most modern texts add to the opening description a bed, a book, at least one candle, and the trunk from which Iachimo emerges, and they often mention that Imogen is in a nightdress and is wearing the bracelet Posthumus gave her, that Iachimo has a notepad and writing instrument, and that there is a striking clock.

Sometimes directions are omitted altogether, especially for disguises. Posthumus has to be a quick-change artist during the opening of Act Five, yet no direct notes are given for his original clothing. Thus though Ff's

> Ile disrobe me
> Of these Italian weedes, and suite my selfe
> As do's a Britaine Pezant.
>
> (p. 109, ll. 5.1.28–30)

allows us to realise he enters dressed as a Roman invader, there is no later direction to the fact of his changing, nor any indication in any of the following three entries set for him as to how he is dressed. Seeking death for his wrongful treatment of Imogen, it is not until Act Five Scene 3 that the reader realises he had been dressed as a Briton during the previous two appearances, but has now changed back into Italian garb in the hope of being captured and killed by the victorious British. In his passion, the lines about his costume changes almost slide by unrecognised

> I have resum'd againe
> The part I came in.
>
> (p. 114, ll. 5.3.91–2)

Thankfully, most modern texts are very careful to explain how he is dressed throughout the opening scenes of Act Five.

MODERN TEXT INVENTIONS

Sometimes modern texts do excellent detective work, and add directions for actions which would be missed by all but the most seasoned of theatrical practitioners. In the above first change of clothing speech for Posthumus, since there is so little time for him between the moment in the speech when the remark is made and his next entry, a few modern texts make the sensible suggestion he will have to change costume during the speech, something only a costume designer or a very experienced director would normally notice.

However, sometimes the added stage directions should be taken with a grain of salt. For example, knowing of Cornelius' dislike and mistrust of the Queene, would he give her the drugs immediately, as some modern texts suggest (p. 19, footnote #3 for l. 1.6.8), or wait until the last possible moment, surrendering them only after the Queene has made it abundantly clear she wants them, perhaps not giving them to her until the end of his speech, ll. 1.6.34–37, p. 20?

In all these cases, this text will footnote the modern texts' additional stage directions, and annotate those which may give problems, or for which there may be alternative readings.

SONGS

Those interested in the genesis and accurate recording of the songs in the play should explore Appendix C in the Arden Shakespeare *Cymbeline*, (op. cit.) pp. 212–16.

TITLE

There is an inconsistency concerning the title by which the play should be known. In the frontispiece to the First Folio, the play is entitled 'Cymbeline King of Britaine', while the header at the beginning of the play itself calls it 'The Tragedie of Cymbeline' (at the top of its thirty-two pages, 'Tragedie' is spelled fourteen times with the 'ie' ending and eighteen times with a 'y'). Modern texts tend to simplify matters by simply calling the play 'Cymbeline', which may be unnecessarily emphasising a character who only speaks 8 percent of the lines of the play, especially when compared with his daughter Imogen, who has 16 percent of the lines. Faced with the two titles, this text will combine them into the formal title of 'The Tragedie of Cymbeline King of Britaine', but, within the body of the text, will adopt the shorter F1 header for the top of each page.

LAST PAGE

Finally: Commentators suggest Compositor B set more than half the text, including the bulk of this play and its last page. Whether intentional or not, a rather wry comment on the whole process is set into this last textual page of the First Folio. Numerically it should read as p. 399. B has set it as 993, perhaps a personal comment on the enormity of the work undertaken.

ACT, SCENE, AND LINE DIVISION

The First Folio Act and Scene division is complete, and adopted by most modern texts with some slight modification.

Neil Freeman,
Vancouver, B.C.
Canada, 1997

RECOMMENDED MODERN TEXTS WITH EXCELLENT SCHOLARLY FOOTNOTES AND RESEARCH

The footnotes in this text are concise, and concentrate either on matters theatrical or choices in word or line structure which distinguish most modern editions and this Folio based text. Items of literary, historical, and linguistic concern have been well researched and are readily available elsewhere. One of the best **research** works in recent years is

Wells, Stanley, and Gary Taylor, eds. *William Shakespeare: A Textual Companion*. Oxford: Clarendon Press, 1987.

In terms of modern **texts,** readers are urged to consult at least one of the following:

Evans, Gwynne Blakemore, Harry Levin, Anne Barton, Herschel Baker, Frank Kermode, Hallet D. Smith, and Marie Edel, eds. *The Riverside Shakespeare*. Copyright © 1974 by Houghton Mifflin Company.

Nosworthy, J. M., ed. *Cymbeline — The Arden Shakespeare*. London: Methuen & Co. Ltd. 1962.

THE TRAGEDIE OF CYMBELINE, KING OF BRITAINE
Dramatis Personæ

CYMBELINE, King of Britaine
MEMBERS OF HIS COURT
the Princesse IMOGEN, (later in disguise as the boy Fidele)
secretly married to Posthumus
HELENE, a lady attending on Imogen

QUEENE, second wife to Cymbeline and
step-mother to Imogen

the Lord CLOTEN, her son

POSTHUMUS Leonatus, a poor gentleman
secretly married to Imogen

Pisanio, his servant

CORNELIUS, a Doctor
2 GENTLEMEN
2 LORDS, attending on Cloten
2 British Captaines   2 Gaolers
LIVING AS OUTCASTS IN THE ENGLISH COUNTRYSIDE
BELARIUS, once known as Morgan, a Lord banished from
Cymbeline's Court, who thereupon stole
Cymbeline's 2 sons when infants

GUIDERIUS, known as Polidore
ARVIRAGUS, known as Cadwal } sons to Cymbeline

IN ITALY
PHILARIO, a friend of Posthumus
Iachimo, an Italian
a FRENCHMAN, a DUTCHMAN, a SPANIARD

ROMANS IN ENGLAND
Caius LUCIUS, initially a Roman Ambassador, later
General of the Invading Roman Army
a Roman CAPTAINE
Philharmonius, a SOOTHSAYER

APPARITIONS APPEARING TO POSTHUMUS LEONATUS
the ghost of his father, SICILIUS Leonatus
the ghost of his Mother
the ghosts of his two Brothers
JUPITER

Lords attending on Cymbeline
Ladies attending on the Queene
Musitians attending on Cloten
Roman Senators and Tribunes

Officers, Captains, Soldiers, Other Attendants

This Cast List has been specially prepared for this edition, and will not be found in any Folio text

THE TRAGEDIE OF

CYMBELINE

Actus Primus.   Scœna Prima

ENTER TWO GENTLEMEN

1st . Gentleman	You do not meet a man but Frownes.
	Our bloods° no more obey the Heavens
	Then our Courtiers : °→ [1]

5

Still seeme, as do's the Kings. [2]
}

2nd . Gentleman	But what's the matter?

1st . Gentleman	His daughter, and the heire of's kingdome (whom
	He purpos'd to his wives sole Sonne, a Widdow
	That late he married) hath referr'd her selfe
	Unto a poore, but worthy Gentleman.

10

                              She's wedded,

Her Husband banish'd ; she imprison'd, all
Is outward sorrow, though I thinke the King
Be touch'd at very heart.
}

15

2nd . Gentleman	None but the King?

1st . Gentleman	He that hath lost her too : so is the Queene,
	That most desir'd the Match.

                         But not a Courtier,

Although they weare their faces to the bent

20

Of the Kings lookes, hath a heart that is not
Glad at the thing they scowle at.
}

2nd . Gentleman	And why so?

[SP 1] this is as set in Ff: however, as the symbol ° shows, most modern editions reduce the three lines to two, arguing the ornate four line high letter 'Y' which opens the text did not allow sufficient space for metrically correct lines to be printed: however, the existing short lines could offer useful pauses as (at least) one court character discusses the 'peculiarity' of the admired Posthumus' banishment

[W 2] Ff = 'Kings', most modern texts = 'King'

1st. Gentleman	He that hath miss'd the Princesse, is a thing
	Too bad, for bad report: and he that hath her,
	(I meane, that married her, alacke good man,
	And therefore banish'd) is a Creature, such,
	As to seeke through the Regions of the Earth
	For one, his like; there would be something failing
	In him, that should compare.
	I do not thinke,
	So faire an Outward, and such stuffe Within
	Endowes a man, but hee.
2nd. Gentleman	You speake him farre.
1st. Gentleman	I do extend him (Sir) within himselfe,
	Crush him together, rather then unfold
	His measure duly.
2nd. Gentleman	What's his name, and Birth?
1st. Gentleman	I cannot delve him to the roote: His Father
	Was call'd Sicillius, who did joyne his Honor
	Against the Romanes, with Cassibulan,[1]
	But had his Titles by Tenantius, whom
	He serv'd with Glory, and admir'd Successe:
	So gain'd the Sur-addition, Leonatus.
	And had (besides this Gentleman in question)
	Two other Sonnes, who in the Warres o'th'time
	Dy'de with their Swords in hand.
	For which, their Father
	Then old, and fond of yssue, tooke such sorrow
	That he quit Being; and his gentle Lady
	Bigge of this Gentleman (our Theame) deceast
	As he was borne.
	The King he takes the Babe
	To his protection, cals him Posthumus Leonatus,
	Breedes him, and makes him of his Bed-chamber,
	Puts to him all the Learnings that his time
	Could make him the receiver of, which he tooke
	As we do ayre, fast as 'twas ministred,
	And in's Spring, became a Harvest: Liv'd in Court
	(Which rare it is to do) most prais'd, most lov'd,
	A sample to the yongest: to th'more Mature,
	A glasse that feated them: and to the graver,
	A Childe that guided Dotards.

L 369 - b

---

[1] F1 = 'Cassibulan', F2 and most modern texts = 'Cassibelan', following the source material

To his Mistris,
(For whom he now is banish'd) her owne price
65 Proclaimes how she esteem'd him; and his Vertue

By her electiõ [1] may be truly read,° what kind of man he is.

2nd. Gentleman I honor him, °even out of your report.

But pray you tell me,° is she sole childe to'th'King?

1st. Gentleman His onely childe: ° [2]

70 He had two Sonnes (if this be worth your hearing,
Marke it) the eldest of them, at three yeares old
I'th'swathing cloathes, the other from their Nursery
Were stolne, and to this houre, no ghesse in knowledge

Which way they went.

75 **2nd. Gentleman** How long is this ago?

1st. Gentleman Some twenty yeares. [3]

2nd. Gentleman That a Kings Children should be so convey'd,
So slackely guarded, and the search so slow
That could not trace them.

80 **1st. Gentleman** Howsoere, 'tis strange,
Or that the negligence may well be laugh'd at:
Yet is it true Sir.

2nd. Gentleman I do well beleeve you.

1st. Gentleman We must forbeare.
85 Heere comes the Gentleman,
The Queene, and Princesse.

[Exeunt]

[AB] [1] most modern texts = 'election' (the source texts had insufficient space to print the complete word)

[LS] [2] this is as set in Ff: however, as the symbol ° shows, most modern editions have relineated the original
irregular structure: Ff show 4 lines of 16/10 or 11/11/4 syllables respectively, the modern texts regularise the
4 lines to 10/10/11 or 12/10: however, the shock value of the original (with the extra long line giving a final
emphatic flourish to the first long speech and the short line giving both characters pause to ponder the new
information) may be preferable on the rehearsal/performance floor

[S] [3] the actor has choice as to which two of these three short lines may be joined as one line of split verse

Scena Secunda

[Many modern texts do not set this as a separate scene, arguing the action is continuous]

ENTER THE QUEENE, POSTHUMUS, AND IMOGEN

Queene	No, be assur'd you shall not finde me (Daughter)
	After the slander of most Step-Mothers,
	Evill-ey'd unto you.
	You're my Prisoner, but
5	Your Gaoler shall deliver you the keyes R 369 - b
	That locke up your restraint.
	For you Posthumus,
	So soone as I can win th'offended King,
	I will be knowne your Advocate: marry yet
10	The fire of Rage is in him, and 'twere good
	You lean'd unto his Sentence, with what patience
	Your wisedome may informe you.
Posthumus	'Please your Hignesse,°
	I will from hence to day.
15 **Queene**	You know the perill: °¹
	Ile fetch a turne about the Garden, pittying
	The pangs of barr'd Affections, though the King
	Hath charg'd you should not speake together.

[Exit]

Imogen	O dissembling Curtesie!
20	How fine this Tyrant
	Can tickle where she wounds?
	My deerest Husband,
	I something feare my Fathers wrath, but nothing
	(Always reserv'd my holy duty) what
25	His rage can do on me.
	You must be gone,
	And I shall heere abide the hourely shot
	Of angry eyes: not comforted to live,
	But that there is this Jewell in the world,

R 369 / L 370 - b : 1.1.70 - 1.1.91

LS ₁
arguing white space was responsible for the printing of these 4 short lines, most modern texts reduce
them to 2 as shown by the symbol °: however, the potential gaps of Ff which surround Posthumus'
enormous decision to leave seem well worth exploring

30		That I may see againe.
	Posthumus	My Queene, my Mistris:
		O Lady, weepe no more, least I give cause
		To be suspected of more tendernesse
		Then doth become a man.
35		I will remaine
		The loyall'st husband, that did ere plight troth.

My residence in Rome, at one Filorio's,[1]
Who, to my Father was a Friend, to me
Knowne but by Letter; thither write (my Queene)
And with mine eyes, Ile drinke the words you send,
Though Inke be made of Gall.

ENTER QUEENE

Queene Be briefe, I pray you:
If the King come, I shall incurre, I know not
How much of his displeasure: [2] yet Ile move him
To walke this way: I never do him wrong,
But he do's buy my Injuries, to be Friends:
Payes deere for my offences. [3]

Posthumus Should we be taking leave
As long a terme as yet we have to live,
The loathnesse to depart, would grow: Adieu.

Imogen Nay, stay a little:
Were you but riding forth to ayre your selfe,
Such parting were too petty.
Looke heere (Love)
This Diamond was my Mothers; take it (Heart)
But keepe it till you woo another Wife,
When Imogen is dead.

Posthumus How, how?
Another?

You gentle Gods, give me but this I have,
And seare up my embracements from a next,
With bonds of death. [4]
Remaine, remaine thou heere,

---

[1] Ff = 'Filorio', most modern texts = 'Philario'

[2] most modern texts indicate this is spoken as an aside

[3] most modern texts add a stage direction giving the 'Queene' an exit

[4] most modern texts add that here Imogen puts a ring upon Posthumus' finger

		While sense can keepe it on: And sweetest, fairest,
65		As I (my poore selfe) did exchange for you
		To your so infinite losse; so in our trifles
		I still winne of you.
		For my sake weare this,
		It is a Manacle of Love, Ile place it
70		Upon this fayrest Prisoner. [1]
	Imogen	O the Gods!
		When shall we see againe?

ENTER CYMBELINE, AND LORDS

	Posthumus	Alacke, the King.
	Cymbeline	Thou basest thing, avoyd hence, from my sight:
75		If after this command thou fraught the Court
		With thy unworthinesse, thou dyest.
		Away,
		Thou'rt poyson to my blood.
80	**Posthumus**	The Gods protect you,
		And blesse the good Remainders of the Court:
		I am gone.

L 370 - b

[Exit]

	Imogen	There cannot be a pinch[†2] in death
		More sharpe then this is.
	Cymbeline	O disloyall thing,
85		That should'st repaye my youth, thou heap'st
		A yeares age on mee.
	Imogen	I beseech you Sir,
		Harme not your selfe with your vexation,
		I am senselesse of your Wrath; a Touch more rare
90		Subdues all pangs, all feares.
	Cymbeline	Past Grace?
		Obedience?
	Imogen	Past hope, and in dispaire, that way past Grace.
	Cymbeline	That might'st have had →[3]
95		The sole Sonne of my Queene.

L 370 - b / R 370 - b : 1.1.118 - 1.1.138

[SD 1] most modern texts suggest that here Posthumus fastens a bracelet around Imogen's arm

[W 2] F1 = 'p inch', F2 = 'pinch'

[S P 3] these two short Ff lines are turned into one split verse line in most modern texts, though the enormity of Cymbeline's reaction well warrants the potential pauses of the original layout

Imogen	O blessed, that I might not: I chose an Eagle,
	And did avoyd a Puttocke.

Cymbeline	Thou took'st a Begger, would'st have made my
	Throne,° a Seate for basenesse.
Imogen	No, I rather added° a lustre to it.
Cymbeline	O thou vilde one!
Imogen	Sir,° [1]

	It is your fault that I have lov'd Posthumus:
	You bred him as my Play-fellow, and he is
	A man, worth any woman: Over-buyes mee
	Almost the summe he payes.
	}
Cymbeline	What? art thou mad?
Imogen	Almost Sir: Heaven restore me: would I were
	A Neat-heards Daughter, and my Leonatus
	Our Neighbour-Shepheards Sonne.

ENTER QUEENE

Cymbeline	Thou foolish thing; [2]
	They were againe together: you have done
	Not after our command.
	Away with her,
	And pen her up.
	}
Queene	Beseech your patience: Peace
	Deere Lady daughter, peace.
	Sweet Soveraigne,
	Leave us to our selves, and make your self some comfort
	Out of your best advice.
	}
Cymbeline	Nay let her languish
	A drop of blood a day, and being aged
	Dye of this Folly.

[Exit]

ENTER PISANIO

LS[1] this is as set in Ff: however, as the symbol ° shows, most modern editions reduce the five irregular lines (9/6/11/4/1 syllables) to three of almost metric regularity (10/11/10): however, the original layout offers great irregularity as father and daughter argue (with the possibility even that the lines are spoken one on top of another) instead of in the modern purer arrangement so suggestive of self-control

WHO[2] most modern texts suggest Cymbeline's first phrase is to Imogen, then he switches to talk to the Queene: F1's lack of directions offers the possibility that the insult is also to the Queen, and not Imogen at all

Queene		Fye, you must give way:
125		Heere is your Servant.
		How now Sir?
		What newes?
Pisanio		My Lord your Sonne, drew on my Master.
		}
Queene		Hah?
130		No harme I trust is done?
		}
Pisanio		There might have beene,
		But that my Master rather plaid, then fought,
		And had no helpe of Anger: they were parted
		By Gentlemen, at hand.
		}
135	**Queene**	I am very glad on't.
Imogen		Your Son's my Fathers friend, he takes his part
		To draw upon an Exile.
		O brave Sir,
		I would they were in Affricke both together,
140		My selfe by with a Needle, that I might pricke
		The goer backe.
		Why came you from your Master?
Pisanio		On his command: he would not suffer mee
		To bring him to the Haven: left these Notes
145		Of what commands I should be subject too,
		When't pleas'd you to employ me.
		}
Queene		This hath beene
		Your faithfull Servant: I dare lay mine Honour
		He will remaine so.
150	**Pisanio**	I humbly thanke your Highnesse. R 370 - b
Queene		Pray walke a-while.
		}
Imogen		¹ About some halfe houre hence,

> Pray you speake with me;
> You shall (at least)° go see my Lord aboord.
> 155 For this time leave me. ° ²

[Exeunt]

1R 370 - b / L 371 - b : 1.1.159 - 1.1.178

^{WHO}₁ most modern texts indicate Imogen is addressing Pisanio: also, Ff set the opening of her speech as two
short lines, allowing time for the Queene to withdraw or exit: most modern texts join the two lines together

^{LS}₂ the modern reduction of Ff's three irregular lines (5/10/5 syllables) to two, almost metrically correct lines
(9/11, shown by the symbol °), reduces the possibility of Imogen trying to get some form of silent
message to Pisanio (possibly about seeing Posthumus leave) before having to speak the thought aloud

Scena Tertia

[Most modern texts refer this to this as Act One, Scene 2]

ENTER CLOTTEN, AND TWO LORDS [1]

1st. Lord		Sir, I would advise you to shift a Shirt; the Vio- lence of Action hath made you reek as a Sacrifice: where ayre comes out, ayre comes in: There's none abroad so wholesome as that you vent.
5	**Cloten**	If my Shirt were bloody, then to shift it. Have I hurt him?
	2nd. Lord	No faith: not so much as his patience.
	1st. Lord	Hurt him? His bodie's a passable Carkasse if he bee
10		not hurt. It is a through-fare for Steele if it [2] be not hurt.
	2nd. Lord	His Steele was in debt, it went o'th'Backe-side the Towne.
	Cloten	The Villaine would not stand me.
15	**2nd. Lord**	No, but he fled forward still, toward your face.
	1st. Lord	Stand you? you have Land enough of your owne: But he added to your having, gave you some ground.
	2nd. Lord	As many Inches, as you have Oceans (Puppies.)
	Cloten	I would they had not come betweene us.
20	**2nd. Lord**	So would I, till you had measur'd how long a Foole you were upon the ground.

L 371 - b : 1.2.1 - 1.2.24

WHO *NP* [1] most modern texts show the first Lord as speaking directly to Cloten and the second often atlking in
asides: they also show all three characters to be speaking prose: however, there is the possibility that in
some of the second Lord's lines the first part could be spoken to Cloten (e.g. lines #6 and #15) - and
some of his speeches could be in verse (as could one from the 1st. Lord) as shown with the vertical line
alongside

W [2] Ff = 'it', some modern texts = 'he'

Cloten	And that shee should love this Fellow, and re- fuse mee.
2nd. Lord	If it be a sin to make a true election, she is damn'd.
1st. Lord	Sir, as I told you alwayes: herBeauty & her Braine go not together. Shee's a good signe, but I have seene small reflection of her wit.
2nd. Lord	She shines not upon Fooles, least the reflection Should hurt her.
Cloten	Come Ile to my Chamber: would there had beene some hurt done.
2nd. Lord	I wish not so, unlesse it had bin the fall of an Asse, which is no great hurt.
Cloten	You'l go with us?
1st. Lord	Ile attend your Lordship.
Cloten	Nay come, let's go together.
2nd. Lord	Well my Lord.

25

30

35

[Exeunt]

Scena Quarta

[Most modern editions call this Act One Scene 3]

ENTER IMOGEN, AND PISANIO

Imogen	I would thou grew'st unto the shores o'th'Haven,
	And questioned'st [1] every Saile: if he should write,
	And I not have it, 'twere a Paper lost
	As offer'd mercy is: What was the last
5	That he spake to thee?
Pisanio	It was his Queene, his Queene. ⟩
Imogen	Then wav'd his Handkerchiefe?
Pisanio	And kist it, Madam. ⟩
Imogen	Senselesse Linnen, happier therein then I:
10	And that was all?
Pisanio	No Madam: for so long ⟩
	As he could make me with his [2] eye, or eare,
	Distinguish him from others, he did keepe
	The Decke, with Glove, or Hat, or Handkerchife,
15	Still waving, as the fits and stirres of's mind
	Could best expresse how slow his Soule sayl'd on,
	How swift his Ship.
Imogen	Thou should'st have made him ⟩
	As little as a Crow, or lesse, ere left
20	To after-eye him.
Pisanio	Madam, so I did. ⟩
Imogen	I would have broke mine eye-strings;
	Crack'd them,° but to looke upon him, till the diminution° [3]

L 371 - b

L 371 - b / R 371 - b : 1.3.1 - 1.3.18

W [1] Ff = 'questioned'st', most modern texts = 'question'st' thus maintaining the iambic pentameter

W [2] Ff = 'his', one modern gloss = 'this'

LS [3] Ff's two irregular lines (7/14 syllables) show the emotional struggle Imogen is going through, with both a need-for-breath short line and then a subsequent uncontrolled onrush: most modern texts reduce the moment (9/12 syllables) as shown

		Of space, had pointed him sharpe as my Needle:
25		Nay, followed him, till he had melted from
		The smalnesse of a Gnat, to ayre: and then
		Have turn'd mine eye, and wept.
		But good Pisanio,

When shall we heare from him.

| 30 | **Pisanio** | Be assur'd Madam, →[1] |

With his next vantage.

	Imogen	I did not take my leave of him, but had
		Most pretty things to say: Ere I could tell him
		How I would thinke on him at certaine houres,
35		Such thoughts, and such: Or I could make him sweare,
		The Shees of Italy should not betray
		Mine Interest, and his Honour: or have charg'd him
		At the sixt houre of Morne, at Noone, at Midnight,
		T'encounter me with Orisons, for then
40		I am in Heaven for him: Or ere I could,
		Give him that parting kisse, which I had set
		Betwixt two charming words, comes in my Father,
		And like the Tyrannous breathing of the North,
		Shakes all our buddes from growing.

ENTER A LADY

| 45 | **Lady** | The Queene (Madam)→[2] |
| | | Desires your Highnesse Company. |

	Imogen	Those things I bid you do, get them dispatch'd,
		I will attend the Queene.
		}

| | **Pisanio** | Madam, I shall. |

[Exeunt]

[SP1] most modern texts print these two short lines as one split line, allowing Imogen the pause before lamenting her inadequate farewells: however, Ff's three short lines seem also to allow Pisanio his moment as he wonders how to voice the reply both he and Imogen would like to believe

[SP2] most modern texts join this to Imogen's previous line to form a split verse line: however, Ff's layout allows for more interruption from the Lady (who after all may well be a spy for the Queene)

Scena Quinta

[Most modern texts call this Act One Scene 4]

**ENTER PHILARIO, IACHIMO: A FRENCHMAN, A DUTCH-
MAN, AND A SPANIARD**

Iachimo	Beleeve it Sir, I have seene him in Britaine; hee
	was then of a Cressent note, expected to prove so woor-
	thy, as since he hath beene allowed the name of.
	But I
	could then have look'd on him, without the help of Ad-
	miration, though the Catalogue of his endowments had
	bin tabled by his side, and I to peruse him by Items.

5

Philario	You speake of him when he was lesse furnish'd,
	then now hee is, with that which makes him both with-
	out[†] and within.

10

Frenchman	I have seene him in France: wee had very ma-
	ny there, could behold the Sunne, with as firme eyes as
	hee.

Iachimo	This matter of marrying his Kings Daughter,
	wherein he must be weighed rather by her valew, then
	his owne, words him (I doubt not) a great deale from the
	matter.

15

Frenchman	And then his banishment.

Iachimo	I, and the approbation of those that weepe this
	lamentable divorce under her colours, are wonderfully
	to extend him, be it but to fortifie her judgement, which
	else an easie battery might lay flat, for taking a Begger
	without lesse quality.
	But how comes it, he is to sojourne
	with you?
	How creepes acquaintance?

20

R 371 - b

25

Philario	His Father and I were Souldiers together, to
	whom I have bin often bound for no lesse then my life.

ENTER POSTHUMUS

		Heere comes the Britaine. [1]
30		Let him be so entertained a-
		mong'st you, as suites with Gentlemen of your knowing,
		to a Stranger of his quality.
		I beseech you all be better
		knowne to this Gentleman, whom I commend to you,
35		as a Noble Friend of mine.
		How Worthy he is, I will
		leave to appeare hereafter, rather then story him in his
		owne hearing.

| 30 | | Heere comes the Britaine. [1] |

Heere comes the Britaine. [1]
    Let him be so entertained a-
mong'st you, as suites with Gentlemen of your knowing,
to a Stranger of his quality.
    I beseech you all be better
knowne to this Gentleman, whom I commend to you,
as a Noble Friend of mine.
    How Worthy he is, I will
leave to appeare hereafter, rather then story him in his
owne hearing.

Frenchman   Sir, we have knowne togither in Orleance.

Posthumus   Since when, I have bin debtor to you for courte-
sies, which I will be ever to pay, and yet pay still.

Frenchman   Sir, you o're-rate my poore kindnesse, I was
glad I did attone my Countryman and you: it had beene
pitty you should have beene put together, with so mortall a purpose, as then each bore, upon importance of so
slight and triviall a nature.

Posthumus   By your pardon Sir, I was then a young Travel-
ler, rather shun'd to go even with what I heard, then in
my every action to be guided by others experiences: but
upon my mended judgement (if I offend [2] to say it is men-
ded†[3]) my Quarrell was not altogether slight.

Frenchman   Faith yes, to be put to the arbiterment of
Swords, and by such two, that would by all likelyhood
have confounded one the other, or have falne both.

Iachimo   Can we with manners, aske what was the difference?

Frenchman   Safely, I thinke, 'twas a contention in pub-
licke, which may (without contradiction) suffer the report.
    It was much like an argument that fell out last
night, where each of us fell in praise of our Country-
Mistresses.
    This Gentleman, at that time vouching (and
upon warrant of bloody affirmation) his to be more
Faire, Vertuous, Wise, Chaste, Constant, Qualified, and

L 372 - e : 1.4.28 - 1.4.60

N [1] most modern texts modernise this to = 'Briton'

W [2] though Ff have no extra words here, some modern texts reverse the meaning by adding 'not'

W [3] F1 = 'men/de d', F2 = 'men/ded'

	lesse attemptible then any, the rarest of our Ladies in Fraunce.
Iachimo	That Lady is not now living; or this Gentlemans opinion by this, worne out.
70 **Posthumus**	She holds her Vertue still, and I my mind.
Iachimo	You must not so farre preferre her, 'fore ours of Italy.
Posthumus	Being so farre provok'd as I was in France: I would abate her nothing, though I professe myselfe her
75	Adorer, not her Friend.
Iachimo	As faire, and as good: a kind of hand in hand comparison, had beene something too faire, and too good for any Lady in Britanie; [1] if she went before others.
	I have seene as that Diamond of yours out-lusters many
80	I have beheld, I could not [2] beleeve she excelled many: but I have not seene the most pretious Diamond that is, nor you the Lady.
Posthumus	I prais'd her, as I rated her: so do I my Stone.
Iachimo	What do you esteeme it at?
85 **Posthumus**	More then the world enjoyes.
Iachimo	Either your unparagon'd Mistris[†3] is dead, or she's out-priz'd by a trifle.
Posthumus	You are mistaken: the one may be solde or given, or if there were wealth enough for the purchases, or
90	merite for the guift.
	The other is not a thing for sale, and onely the guift of the Gods.
Iachimo	Which the Gods have given you?
Posthumus	Which by their Graces I will keepe.
95 **Iachimo**	You may weare her in title yours: but you know strange Fowle light upon neighbouring Ponds.

L 372 - e

L 372 - e / R 372 - e : 1.4.60 - 1.4.89

[w1] Ff set a variation of 'Britainie', one gloss offers 'Britaine'

[w2] though Ff have no extra words here, some modern texts add 'but'

[w3] F2 and most modern texts = 'Mistris', F1 = 'Mistirs'

Your Ring may be stolne too, so your brace of unprize-
able Estimations, the one is but fraile, and the other Casu-
all; . [1]

100   A cunning Thiefe, or a (that way) accomplish'd
Courtier, would hazzard the winning both of first and
last.

Posthumus   Your Italy, containes none so accomplish'd a
Courtier to convince the Honour of my Mistris : if in the
105   holding or losse of that, you terme her fraile, I do nothing doubt you have store of Theeves, not withstanding
I feare not my Ring.

Philario   Let us leave heere, Gentlemen?

Posthumus   Sir, with all my heart.
110   This worthy Signior I
thanke him, makes no stranger of me, we are familiar at
first.

Iachimo   With five times so much conversation, I should
get ground of your faire Mistris ; make her go backe, e-
115   ven to the yeilding, had I admittance, and opportunitie
to friend.

Posthumus   No, no.

Iachimo   I dare thereupon pawne the moytie of my E-
state, to your Ring, which in my opinion o're-values it
120   something : but I make my wager rather against your
Confidence, then her Reputation.
                  And to barre your of-
fence heerein to, I durst attempt it against any Lady in
the world.

125 **Posthumus**   You are a great deale abus'd in too bold a per-
swasion, and I doubt not you sustaine what y'are worthy
of, by your Attempt.

Iachimo   What's that?[†2]

Posthumus   A Repulse though your Attempt (as you call
130   it) deserve more ; a punishment too.

[PCT]1 F1 sets two pieces of punctuation: F2 and most modern texts omit the semi-colon

[W]2 F1 = 'rhat', F2 = 'that'

Philario	Gentlemen enough of this, it came in too so- dainely, let it dye as it was borne, and I pray you be bet- ter acquainted.
Iachimo	Would I had put my Estate,^{†1} and my Neighbors on th'approbation of what I have spoke,²
Posthumus	What Lady would you chuse to assaile?
Iachimo	Yours, whom in constancie you thinke stands so safe. I will lay you ten thousands³ Duckets to your Ring, that commend me to the Court where your La- dy is, with no more advantage then the opportunitie of a second conference, and I will bring from thence, that Honor of hers, which you imagine so reserv'd.
Posthumus	I will wage against your Gold, Gold to it: My Ring I holde deere as my finger, 'tis part of it.^{†4}
Iachimo	You are a Friend,⁵ and there in⁶ the wiser: if you buy Ladies flesh at a Million a Dram, you cannot pre- serve^{†7} it from tainting; but I see you have some Religion in you, that you feare.
Posthumus	This is but a custome in your tongue: you beare a graver purpose I hope.
Iachimo	I am the Master of my speeches, and would under- go what's spoken, I sweare.

Posthumus	Will you?
	       I shall but lend my Diamond till
	your returne: let there be Covenants drawne between's.
	My Mistris exceedes in goodnesse, the hugenesse of your
	unworthy thinking.
	         I dare you to this match: heere's my
	Ring.

135

140

145

150

155

160

R 372 - e : 1.4.120 - 1.4.146

^W₁ F1 = 'Fstate', F2 = 'Estate'

^{RCT}₂ set as a comma in F1 (perhaps suggesting an interruption by Posthumus' next speech), F2 and most
modern texts print the final punctuation as a regular period

^W₃ F1-2 = 'thousands', F3 and most modern texts = 'thousand'

^W₄ F1 = 'i t', F2 = 'it'

^W₅ though most modern texts agree with Ff and print this as 'a Friend', one interesting gloss = 'afraid'

^W₆ F1 = 'there in', F2/most modern texts = 'therein'

^W₇ F2 and most modern texts = 'preserve', F1 = 'presevre'

Philario	I will have it no lay.
Iachimo	By the Gods it is one: if I bring you no suffi-
	cient testimony that I have enjoy'd the deerest bodily
165		part of your Mistris: my ten thousand Duckets are yours,
	so is your Diamond too: if I come off, and leave her in
	such honour as you have trust in; Shee your Jewell, this
	your Jewell, and my Gold are yours: provided, I have
	your commendation, for my more free entertainment.
170 **Posthumus**	I embrace these Conditions, let us have Articles
	betwixt us: onely thus farre you shall answere, if you
	make your voyage upon her, and give me directly to un-
	derstand, you have prevayl'd, I am no further your Ene-
	my† shee is not worth our debate.
175		If shee remaine unse-
	duc'd, you not making it appeare otherwise: for your ill
	opinion, and th'assault you have made to her chastity, you
	shall answer me with your Sword.
Iachimo	Your hand, a Covenant: wee will have these
180		things set downe by lawfull Counsell, and straightaway
	for Britaine, least the Bargaine should catch colde, and
	sterve: I will fetch my Gold, and have our two Wagers
	recorded.
Posthumus	Agreed. [1]
185 **Frenchman**	Will this hold, thinke you.
Philario	Signior Iachimo will not from it.
	Pray let us follow 'em.

R 372 - e

[Exeunt]

R 372 - e / L 373 - b : 1.4.147 - 1.4.172

[SD] [1] most modern texts add a stage direction here for the exits of Posthumus and Iachimo, (usually in separate directions)

Scena Sexta.

[Most modern texts call this Act One Scene 5]

ENTER QUEENE, LADIES, AND CORNELIUS

Queene	Whiles yet the dewe's on ground,
	Gather those Flowers, °
	Make haste.
	Who ha's the note of them?
Lady [1]	I Madam. ° [2]

| Queene | Dispatch. |

[Exit Ladies]

	Now Master Doctor, have you brought those drugges?
Cornelius	Pleaseth your Highnes, I: here they are, Madam: [3]
	But I beseech your Grace, without offence
	(My Conscience bids me aske) wherefore you have
	Commanded of me these most poysonous Compounds,
	Which are the moovers of a languishing death:
	But though slow, deadly.
	}
Queene	I wonder, Doctor,
	Thou ask'st me such a Question: Have I not bene
	Thy Pupill long?
	Hast thou not learn'd me how
	To make Perfumes?
	Distill?
	Preserve?
	Yea so,
	That our great King himselfe doth woo me oft
	For my Confections?

[P][1] this could be the same Lady who interrupted Imogen and Pisanio at the end of Act 1 Scene 4

[LS][2] most modern editions reduce Ff's four short lines (6/4 or 5/8/3 syllables respectively) to two almost poetically correct lines (10 or 11/11): as a consequence the potential care and/or ritual of the original is lost

[SD][3] most modern texts add the stage direction that this is where Cornelius dutifully hands a box of drugs to the Queene: this seems a little unnecessary - what if he tries to keep them to himself for a while longer? and what if she has to take them from him (or make him give them to her) later in the speech: Ff's lack of stage direction allows for many possibilities

	Having thus farre proceeded,
25		(Unlesse thou think'st me divellish) is't not meete
	That I did amplifie my judgement in
	Other Conclusions?
	I will try the forces
	Of these thy Compounds, on such Creatures as
30		We count not worth the hanging (but none humane)
	To try the vigour of them, and apply
	Allayments to their Act, and by them gather
	Their severall vertues, and effects. }

Cornelius	Your Highnesse
35		Shall from this practise, but make hard your heart:
	Besides, the seeing these effects will be
	Both noysome, and infectious. }

| **Queene** | O content thee. |

ENTER PISANIO

	[1] Heere comes a flattering Rascall, upon him
40		Will I first worke: Hee's[2] for his Master,
	And enemy to my Sonne.
	How now Pisanio?
	Doctor, your service for this time is ended,
	Take your owne way. }

L 373 - b

45	**Cornelius**	I do suspect you, Madam,
	But you shall do no harme. [3] }

| **Queene** | Hearke thee, a word. [4] |

Cornelius	[5] I do not like her.
	She doth thinke she ha's
50		Strange ling'ring poysons: I do know her spirit,
	And will not trust one of her malice with
	A drugge of such damn'd Nature.
	Those she ha's,
	Will stupifie and dull the Sense a-while,
55 | | Which first (perchance) shee'l prove on Cats and Dogs, |

L 373 - b / R 373 - b : 1.5.15 - 1.5.38

[A] 1 most modern texts indicate this is spoken as an aside

[W] 2 though Ff have no extra words here, some modern texts add the word 'factor'

[A] 3 most modern texts indicate this is spoken as an aside

[WHO] 4 most modern texts suggest that here the Queene is talking to Pisanio

[A] 5 most modern texts suggest Cornelius continues his aside

Then afterward up higher: but there is
No danger in what shew of death it makes,
More then the locking up the Spirits a time,
To be more fresh, reviving.
                         She is fool'd
With a most false effect: and I, the truer,
So to be false with her.

Queene   No further service, Doctor, $\}$
Untill I send for thee.

Cornelius   I humbly take my leave. $\}$

                      [Exit]

Queene   Weepes she still (saist thou?) $\rightarrow$[1]
Dost thou thinke in time
She will not quench, and let instructions enter
Where Folly now possesses?
                      Do thou worke:
When thou shalt bring me word she loves my Sonne,
Ile tell thee on the instant, thou art then
As great as is thy Master: Greater, for
His Fortunes all lye speechlesse, and his name
Is at last gaspe.
                Returne he cannot, nor
Continue where he is: To shift his being,
Is to exchange one misery with another,
And every day that comes, comes to decay
A dayes worke[2] in him.
                What shalt thou expect
To be depender on a thing that leanes?

Who cannot be new built, nor ha's no Friends
So much, as but to prop him?
               [3] Thou tak'st up
Thou know'st not what: But take it for thy labour,
It is a thing I made, which hath the King
Five times redeem'd from death.
                  I do not know
What is more Cordiall.
               Nay, I prythee take it,

R 373 - b : 1.5.39 - 1.5.64

[SP 1] most modern texts join these two short lines together to form a single ten syllable line; in so doing they lose the potential for Pisanio's non-reply between Ff's two short lines

[W 2] though most modern texts agree with Ff and print this as 'worke', one interesting gloss = 'worth'

[SD 3] most modern texts add the stage direction that the Queene drops the box of drugs given her by Cornelius

It is an earnest of a farther good
That I meane to thee.
　　　　　　　Tell thy Mistris how

95　The case stands with her: doo't, as from thy selfe;
Thinke what a chance thou changest on,[1] but thinke
Thou hast thy Mistris still, to boote, my Sonne,
Who shall take notice of thee.
　　　　　　　Ile move the King

100　To any shape of thy Preferment, such
As thou'lt desire: and then my selfe, I cheefely,
That set thee on to this desert, am bound
To loade thy merit richly.
　　　　　　　Call my women.

[Exit Pisanio]

105　Thinke on my words.[2]
　　　　　　　A slye, and constant knave,
Not to be shak'd: the Agent for his Master,
And the Remembrancer of her, to hold
The hand-fast to her Lord.

110　　　　　　　I have given him that,
Which if he take, shall quite unpeople her
Of Leidgers for her Sweete: and which, she after
Except she bend her humor, shall be assur'd
To taste of too.

ENTER PISANIO, AND LADIES

115　So, so: Well done, well done:
The Violets, Cowslippes, and the Prime-Roses
Beare to my Closset: Fare thee well, Pisanio.

Thinke on my words.

[Exit Queene and Ladies]

Pisanio　And shall do:
120　But when to my good Lord, I prove untrue,
Ile choake my selfe: there's all Ile do for you.

[Exit]

R 373 - b

R 373 - b　:　1.5.65 - 1.5.87

[W] [1] Ff = 'chance thou changest on', most modern texts = either　a) 'change thou chancest on'
　　　　　　　　　　　　　　　　　　　　　　　b) 'chance thou hangest on'

[SD] [2] most modern texts place Pisanio's exit here, half a line later than Ff: this seems somewhat arbitrary, after all the Queene could be calling after him as he leaves

22

Scena Septima

[Most modern texts call this Act One Scene 6]

ENTER IMOGEN ALONE

Imogen	A Father cruell, and a Stepdame false,
	A Foolish Suitor to a Wedded-Lady,[1]
	That hath her Husband banish'd: O, that Husband,
	My supreame Crowne of griefe, and those repeated
5	Vexations of it.
	Had I bin Theefe-stolne,
	As my two Brothers, happy: but most miserable
	Is the desires[2] that's glorious.
	Blessed be those
10	How meane so ere, that have their honest wills,
	Which seasons comfort.
	Who may this be?
	Fye.

ENTER PISANIO, AND IACHIMO

Pisanio	Madam, a Noble Gentleman of Rome,
15	Comes from my Lord with Letters.
	}
Iachimo	Change you, Madam:
	The Worthy Leonatus is in safety,
	And greetes your Highnesse deerely.[3]
	}
Imogen	Thanks good Sir,
20	You're kindly welcome.
Iachimo	All of her, that is out of doore, most rich:
	If she be furnish'd with a mind so rare
	She is alone th'Arabian-Bird; and I
	Have lost the wager.
25	Boldnesse be my Friend:

L 374 - e : 1.6.1 - 1.6.18

[PCT1] F1 shows a faint hyphen: F2 and most modern texts show nothing at all

[W2] F1 = 'desires', F2 and most modern texts = 'desire'

[SD3] here most modern texts add the stage direction of Iachimo giving Imogen a letter

Arme me Audacitie from head to foote,
Or like[†1] the Parthian I shall flying fight,
Rather directly fly. [2]

IMOGEN READS

He is one of the Noblest note, to whose kindnesses I am most in-
30 *finitely tied .*
        Reflect upon him accordingly, as you value your
trust. [3]   Leonatus

So farre I reade aloud.

But even the very middle of my heart
35 Is warm'd by'th'rest, and take[†4] it thankefully.

You are as welcome (worthy Sir) as I
Have words to bid you, and shall finde it so
In all that I can do.
                    }

Iachimo   Thankes fairest Lady:
40 What are men mad?
                  Hath Nature given them eyes
To see this vaulted Arch, and the rich Crop
Of Sea and Land, which can distinguish 'twixt
The firie Orbes above, and the twinn'd Stones
45 Upon the number'd[5] Beach, and can we not
Partition make with Spectacles[†6] so pretious
Twixt faire, and foule?
                }

Imogen   What makes your admiration?

Iachimo   It cannot be i'th'eye: for Apes, and Monkeys
50 'Twixt two such She's, would chatter this way, and
Contemne with mowes the other.
                  Nor i'th'judgment:
For Idiots in this case of favour, would
Be wisely definit: Nor i'th'Appetite.

55 Sluttery to such neate Excellence, oppos'd
Should make desire vomit emptinesse,

L 374 - e : 1.6.19 - 1.6.45

[W1] F1 = 'Orlike', F2 = 'Or like'

[A2] most modern texts indicate this is spoken as an aside

[W3] Ff = 'trust', an occasional modern text = 'truest'

[W4] F1= 'rake', F2 = 'take', most modern texts = 'takes'

[W5] Ff = 'number'd', some modern texts = 'unnumber'd'

[W6] F1 = 'Spectales', F2 = 'Spectacles'

> Not so allur'd[†1] to feed.
>
> **Imogen**   What is the matter trow?
>
> **Iachimo**   The Cloyed will: [2]

60

                  That satiate yet unsatisfi'd desire, that Tub
Both fill'd and running: Ravening first the Lambe,
Longs after for the Garbage.
}

Imogen   What, deere Sir,
Thus rap's you?

65   Are you well?   L 374 - e

Iachimo   Thanks Madam well: [3] Beseech you Sir,
Desire my Man's abode, where I did leave him:
He's strange and peevish.
}

Pisanio   I was going Sir,

70   To give him welcome.

[Exit]

Imogen   Continues well my Lord?

His health beseech you?
}

Iachimo   Well, Madam.

Imogen   Is he dispos'd to mirth?

75   I hope he is.

Iachimo   Exceeding pleasant: none a stranger there,
So merry, and so gamesome: he is call'd
The Britaine Reveller.
}

Imogen   When he was heere

80   He did incline to sadnesse, and oft times
Not knowing[†4] why.
}

Iachimo   I never saw him sad.

There is a Frenchman his Companion, one
An eminent Monsieur, that it seemes much loves

85   A Gallian-Girle at home.

L 374 - e / R 374 - e : 1.6.46 - 1.6.66

[W][1] F1 = 'allur,d', F2 = 'allur'd'

[S][2] the actor has choice as to which two of these three short lines may be joined as one line of split verse

[WHO][3] most modern texts indicate this is addressed to Pisanio

[W][4] F2 and most modern texts = 'knowing', F1 = 'knowiug'

He furnaces
The thicke sighes from him; whiles the jolly Britaine,
(Your Lord I meane) laughes from's free lungs: cries oh,
Can my sides hold, to think that man who knowes
90 By History, Report, or his owne proofe
What woman is, yea what she cannot choose
But must be: ¹ will's free houres languish:
For assured bondage?
                                                    }

Imogen   Will my Lord say so?

95 **Iachimo**   I Madam, with his eyes in flood with laughter,
It is a Recreation to be by

And heare him mocke the Frenchman:
But Heaven's know° some men are much too blame.

Imogen   Not he I hope. °

100 **Iachimo**   Not he:
But yet Heavens bounty towards him, might° ²

Be us'd more thankfully.
                                        In himselfe 'tis much;
In you, which I account ³ his beyond all Talents.

105 Whil'st I am bound to wonder, I am bound
To pitty too.

Imogen   What do you pitty Sir?
                                        }

Iachimo   Two Creatures heartyly.
                                        }

Imogen   Am I one Sir?

110 You looke on me: what wrack discerne you in me
Deserves your pitty?
                                        }

Iachimo   Lamentable: what
To hide me from the radiant Sun, and solace
I'th'Dungeon by a Snuffe.
                                        }

115 **Imogen**   I pray you Sir,
Deliver with more opennesse your answeres
To my demands.

R 374 - e : 1.6.67 - 1.6.89

PCT ₁ F1 sets two heavy pieces of punctuation (a colon each time) surrounding this phrase, suggesting
Iachimo controlling himself (stifling laughter perhaps): F2 softens this by setting a colon then a comma,
while most modern texts set a comma and remove the second piece of punctuation entirely

LS ₂ most modern editions reduce Ff's five irregular lines (7/9 or 10/4/2/8-10) to three almost regular metric lines
(10 or 11/10/10 with elision): unfortunately, the reduction regularises the very tricky moments of Iachimo's
laying in of more bait, and of Imogen's faltering reactions

W ₃ Ff set a twelve syllable line, which some modern texts reduce by replacing Ff's 'account' with 'count'

Why do you pitty me?

Iachimo	That others do,
120	(I was about to say) enjoy your _____ but
	It is an office of the Gods to venge it,
	Not mine to speake on't.

}

Imogen	You do seeme to know
	Something of me, or what concernes me; pray you
125	Since doubting things go ill, often hurts more
	Then to be sure they do.

For Certainties

Either are past remedies; or timely knowing
The remedy then borne.

Discover to me

130   What both you spur and stop.

}

Iachimo	Had I this cheeke
	To bathe my lips upon: this hand, whose touch,
	(Whose every touch) which force the Feelers soule
135	To'th'oath of loyalty. [1]

This object, which

Takes prisoner the wild motion of mine eye,
Fiering[2] it onely heere, should I (damn'd[3] then)   R 374 - e
Slavver with lippes as common as the stayres

140   That mount the Capitoll: Joyne gripes, with hands
Made hard with hourely falshood (falshood as
With labour:) then by peeping in an eye
Base and illustrious as the smoakie light
That's fed with stinking Tallow: it were fit

145   That all the plagues of Hell should at one time
Encounter such revolt.

}

Imogen	My Lord, I feare
	Has forgot Brittaine.

}

Iachimo	And himselfe, not I
150	Inclin'd to this intelligence, pronounce
	The Beggery of his change: but 'tis your Graces
	That from my mutest Conscience, to my tongue,
	Charmes this report out.

}

Imogen	Let me heare no more.

R 374 - e / L 375 - b - : 1.6.89 - 1.6.117

PCT [1] Ff set a period, as if Iachimo needs an extra moment to control himself: most modern texts reduce
the need by setting a colon

W [2] F1-2 and most modern texts = 'Fiering': F3 = 'Fixing'

W [3] Ff = 'damn'd', one modern gloss offers 'dampn'd'

155	**Iachimo**	O deerest Soule: your Cause doth strike my hart
		With pitty, that doth make me sicke.
		A Lady
		So faire, and fasten'd to an Emperie
		Would make the great'st King double, to be partner'd
160		With Tomboyes hyr'd, with that selfe exhibition
		Which your owne Coffers yeeld: with diseas'd ventures
		That play with all Infirmities for Gold,
		Which rottennesse can lend [1] Nature.
		Such boyl'd stuffe
165		As well might poyson Poyson.
		Be reveng'd,
		Or she that bore you, was no Queene, and you
		Recoyle from your great Stocke.
		}
	Imogen	Reveng'd:
170		How should I be reveng'd?
		If this be true,
		(As I have such a Heart, that both mine eares
		Must not in haste abuse) if it be true,
		How should I be reveng'd?
		}
175	**Iachimo**	Should he make me
		Live like Diana's Priest, betwixt cold sheets,
		Whiles he is vaulting variable Rampes
		In your despight, upon your purse: revenge it.
		I dedicate my selfe to your sweet pleasure,
180		More Noble then that runnagate to your bed,
		And will continue fast to your Affection,
		Still close, as sure.
		}
	Imogen	What hoa, Pisanio ?
	Iachimo	Let me my service tender on your lippes.
185	**Imogen**	Away, I do condemne mine eares, that have
		So long attended thee.
		If thou wert Honourable
		Thou would'st have told this tale for Vertue, not
		For such an end thou seek'st, as base, as strange:
190		Thou wrong'st a Gentleman, who is as farre
		From thy report, as thou from Honor: and
		Solicites heere a Lady, that disdaines
		Thee, and the Divell alike.

---

[w] [1] though Ff have no extra words here, some modern texts add 'to', presumably to complete the hexameter: theatrically this may be irrelevant, if not in the way, for Iachimo is now about to strike, and grammatical niceties may not be his prime consideration

What hoa, Pisanio ?

195 The King my Father shall be made acquainted
Of thy Assault : if he shall thinke it fit,
A sawcy Stranger in his Court, to Mart
As in a Romish Stew, and to expound
His beastly minde to us ; he hath a Court
200 He little cares for, and a Daughter, who
He not respects at all.
What hoa, Pisanio ?

Iachimo O happy Leonatus I may say,
The credit that thy Lady hath of thee
205 Deserves thy trust, and thy most perfect goodnesse
Her assur'd credit.
Blessed live you long,
A Lady to the worthiest Sir, that ever
Country call'd his ; and you his Mistris, onely
210 For the most worthiest fit.
Give me your pardon,
I have spoke this to know if your Affiance
Were deeply rooted, and shall make your Lord,   L 375 - b
That which he is, new o're : And he is one
215 The truest manner'd : such a holy Witch,
That he enchants Societies into him :
Halfe all men[1] hearts are his.

Imogen You make amends.

Iachimo He sits 'mongst men, like a defended[2] God ;
220 He hath a kinde of Honor sets him off,
More then a mortall seeming.
Be not angrie
(Most mighty Princesse) that I have adventur'd
To try your taking of a false report, which hath
225 Honour'd with confirmation your great Judgement,
In the election of a Sir, so rare,
Which you know, cannot erre.
The love I beare him,
Made me to fan you thus, but the Gods made you
230 (Unlike all others) chaffelesse.
Pray your pardon.

L 375 - b / R 375 - b : 1.6.148 - 1.6.178

W [1] F1 = 'men', F2 and most modern texts = 'mens'

W [2] F1 and some modern texts = 'defended', F2 and some modern texts = 'descended'

Imogen	All's well Sir: → [1]	
	Take my powre i'th'Court for yours.	
Iachimo	My humble thankes: I had almost forgot	
235	T'intreat your Grace, but in a small request,	
	And yet of moment too, for it concernes:	
	Your Lord, my selfe, and other Noble Friends	
	Are partners in the businesse. }	
Imogen	Pray what is't? †2	
240 **Iachimo**	Some dozen Romanes of us, and your Lord	
	(The³ best Feather of our wing) have mingled summes	
	To buy a Present for the Emperor:	
	Which I (the Factor for the rest) have done	
	In France: 'tis Plate of rare device, and Jewels	
245	Of rich, and exquisite forme, their valewes great,	
	And I am something curious, being strange	
	To have them in safe stowage: May it please you	
	To take them in protection. }	
Imogen	Willingly:	
250	And pawne mine Honor for their safety, since	
	My Lord hath interest in them, I will keepe them	
	In my Bed-chamber. }	
Iachimo	They are in a Trunke	
	Attended by my men: I will make bold	
255	To send them to you, onely for this night:	
	I must aboord to morrow. }	
Imogen	O no, no.	
Iachimo	Yes I beseech: or I shall short my word	
	By length'ning my returne.	
260	From Gallia,	
	I crost the Seas on purpose, and on promise	
	To see your Grace. }	
Imogen	I thanke you for your paines:	
	But not away to morrow. }	
265 **Iachimo**	O I must Madam.	

ˢ ᴾ₁ most modern texts print these two short Ff lines as one complete line: in so doing they rob Imogen of
two potential hesitations, one before accepting Iachimo's pardon, the second before offering him her help

ᵂ ₂ F2 and most modern texts = 'what is't', (F1 = 'whatis't' - almost printing the two words as one)

ᵂ ₃ a few modern texts omit 'The', presumably to reduce the 11 syllable line to metric regularity

Therefore I shall beseech you, if you please
To greet your Lord with writing, doo't to night,
I have out-stood my time, which is materiall
To'th'tender of our Present.

270 **Imogen** I will write:
Send your Trunke to me, it shall safe be kept,
And truely yeelded you: you're very welcome.

[Exeunt]

Actus Secundus. Scena Prima

ENTER CLOTTEN, AND THE TWO LORDS

Cloten	Was there ever man had such lucke? when I kist
	the Jacke upon an up-cast, to be hit away?
	I had a hun-
	dred pound on't: and then a whorson Jacke-an-Apes,
	must take me up for swearing, as if I borrowed mine
	oathes of him, and might not spend them at my pleasure.
1st . Lord	What got he by that? you have broke his pate
	with your Bowle.
2nd . Lord [1]	If his wit had bin like him that broke it: it would
	have run all out.
Cloten	When a Lord is dispos'd to sweare: it is
	not for any standers by to curtall his oathes.
	Ha?
|**2nd . Lord**	No my Lord; nor crop the eares of them.
Cloten	Whorson dog: I gave him satisfaction? would
	he had bin one of my Ranke.
|**2nd . Lord**	To have smell'd like a Foole.
Cloten	I am not vext more at any thing in th'earth: a
	pox on't.
	I had [†2] rather not be so Noble as I am: they dare
	not fight with me, because of the Queene my Mo-
	ther: every Jacke-Slave hath his belly full of Fighting,
	and I must go up and downe like a Cock, that no body
	can match.
|**2nd . Lord**	You are Cocke and Capon too, and you crow
	Cock, with your combe on.

R 375 - b

R 375 - b / L 376 - e : 2.1.1. - 2.1.24

[WA]1 as with his previous scene (Act One Scene 3 this script) most modern texts indicate the major part of
the 2nd Lord's speeches are spoken as asides and that he speaks prose: however, Ff suggest he
occasionally could be speaking verse: such lines will again be marked with a vertical line

[W]2 F1 = 'Ihad', F2 = 'I had'

	Cloten	Sayest thou?
	2nd . Lord	It is not fit you[1] Lordship should undertake every Companion, that you give offence too.
30	**Cloten**	No, I know that: but it is fit I should commit offence to my inferiors.
	2nd . Lord	I, it is fit for your Lordship onely.
	Cloten	Why so I say.
35	**1st . Lord**	Did you heere of a Stranger that's come to Court to [2] night?
	Cloten	A Stranger, and I not know on't?
	2nd . Lord	He's a strange Fellow himselfe, and knowes it not. [3]
	1st . Lord	There's an Italian come, and 'tis thought one of Leonatus Friends.

40	**Cloten**	Leonatus ?
		          A banisht Rascall; and he's another, whatsoever he be.
		                    Who told you of this Stranger?

	1st . Lord	One of your Lordships Pages.
45	**Cloten**	Is it fit I went to looke upon him? Is there no derogation[4] in't?
	2nd . Lord	You cannot derogate my Lord.
	Cloten	Not easily I thinke.
50	**2nd . Lord**	You are a Foole graunted, therefore your Issues being foolish do not derogate. [5]
	Cloten	Come, Ile go see this Italian: what I have lost to day at Bowles, Ile winne to night of him. Come: go.

[w][1] F1-2 = 'you', F3 and most modern texts = 'your'

[w][2] F1 = 'night', F2 and most modern texts = 'to night'

[A][3] most modern texts indicate this is spoken as an aside

[w][4] F1 = 'de₋rogation', F2 = 'derogation'

[A][5] most modern texts indicate this is spoken as an aside

55   **2nd . Lord**   Ile attend your Lordship.

[Exit] [1]

That such a craftie Divell as is his Mother
Should yeild the world this Asse: A woman, that
Beares all downe with her Braine, and this her Sonne,
Cannot take two from twenty for his heart,
60   And †[2] leave eighteene.
                         Alas poore Princesse,
Thou divine Imogen , what thou endur'st,
Betwixt a Father by thy Step-dame govern'd,
A Mother hourely coyning plots: A Wooer,
65   More hatefull then the foule expulsion is
Of thy deere Husband. [3]
                      Then that horrid Act
Of the divorce, heel'd make the Heavens hold firme
The walls of thy deere Honour.
70   Keepe unshak'd
That Temple thy faire mind, that thou maist stand
T'enjoy thy banish'd Lord: and this great Land.

[Exeunt] [4]

[SD][1] most modern texts suggest just Cloten and the 1st. Lord exit, which renders the final Ff stage direction
in the scene 'Exeunt' pointless

[W][2] F2 and most modern texts = 'And' F1 = 'aud'

[PCT][3] this and the next full line raise serious grammatical problems: most modern texts do not reproduce the
F1-3 period (or any punctuation at all) and end the sentence on the next line after 'make' (omitting the
comma between 'divorce' and 'heel'd'): the lines thus read
                 Of thy deere Husband then (i.e. than) that horrid Act
                 Of the divorce heel'd make.
                       The Heavens hold firm
the only (long-shot) justification for keeping the Ff layout is to acknowledge the modern restructuring as
grammatical sense and couple it with such emotional turmoil that the 2nd. Lord's rhetoric momentarily fails;
F4 sets a comma

[SD][4] if the Ff stage direction is maintained then
        a) the modern texts' earlier amplification, footnote #1 above, cannot apply
        b) what are Cloten and the 1st. Lord doing on stage until this group exit?
in fact the group exit could have stemmed from the habits of the acknowledged manuscript copyist Ralph
Crane, who was predisposed to set down group entries at the beginning of scenes, and, more infrequently,
group exits at the end

Scena Secunda

ENTER IMOGEN, IN HER BED, AND A LADY [1]

Imogen	Who's there?
	My woman: Helene?
	}
Lady {Helene} [2]	Please you Madam.
Imogen	What houre is it? L 376 - e
	}
5 **Lady**	Almost midnight, Madam.

Imogen   I have read three houres then: → [3]
Mine eyes are weake,
Fold downe the leafe where I have left: to bed.

Take not away the Taper, leave it burning:
10   And if thou canst awake by foure o'th'clock,
I prythee call me: Sleepe hath ceiz'd me wholly. [4]

To your protection I commend me, Gods,
From Fayries, and the Tempters of the night,
Guard me beseech yee.

[Sleepes]
[Iachimo from the Trunke]

15   **Iachimo**   The Crickets sing, and mans ore-labor'd sense
Repaires it selfe by rest: Our Tarquine thus
Did softly presse the Rushes, ere he waken'd
The Chastitie he wounded.
                  Cytherea,
20   How bravely thou becom'st thy Bed; fresh Lilly,
And whiter then the Sheetes: that I might touch,
But kisse, one kisse.

L 376 - e / R 376 - e : 2.2.1 - 2.2.17

SD [1] most modern texts add that the trunk must be on stage too (either discovered or carried in)

P [2] unlike the other Ladies so far seen gathering flowers with the Queene (Act 1 scene 6 this script, page 19), or interrupting Imogen and Pisanio (Act 1 Scene 4, page 12) this character is given a name: thus it is possible that this is a different Lady from at the very least the one seen conversing with the Queene, unless the reader/actor/director wants to add to the treachery motif throughout the play

SP [3] arguing white space was responsible for the printing of these 2 short lines, most modern texts reduce them to 1: however, there may be a moment for Imogen to try and justify the seemingly irrelevant line about weak eyes (has she been weeping for Posthumus? and wants to explain the watery eyes somehow)

A [4] most modern texts add a stage direction here for Helene to exit

Rubies unparagon'd,
How deerely they[1] doo't: 'Tis her breathing that
25 Perfumes the Chamber thus: the Flame o'th'Taper
Bowes toward her, and would under-peepe her lids.[2]

To see th'inclosed Lights, now Canopied
Under these windowes, White and Azure lac'd
With Blew of Heavens owne tinct.
30   But my designe.

To note the Chamber, I will write all downe,
Such, and such pictures: There the window, such
Th'adornement of her Bed; the Arras, Figures,
Why such, and such: and the Contents o'th'Story.

35 Ah, but some naturall notes about her Body,
Above ten thousand meaner Moveables
Would testifie, t'enrich mine Inventorie.

O sleepe, thou Ape of death, lye dull upon her,
And be her Sense but as a Monument,
40 Thus in a Chappell lying.
                            Come off, come off;[3]
As slippery as the Gordian-knot was hard.

'Tis mine, and this will witnesse outwardly,
As strongly as the Conscience do's within:
45 To'th'madding of her Lord.
                            On her left brest
A mole Cinque-spotted: Like the Crimson drops
I'th'bottome of a Cowslippe.
                            Heere's a Voucher,
50 Stronger then ever Law could make; this Secret
Will force him thinke I have pick'd the lock, and t'ane
The treasure of her Honour.
                            No more: to what end?

55 Why should I write this downe, that's riveted,
Screw'd to my memorie.
                            She hath bin reading late,
The Tale of Tereus, heere the leaffe's turn'd downe
Where Philomele gave up.

W 1
though most modern texts agree with Ff and print this as 'they', one interesting gloss = 'they'd', and in applying the conditional tense to the verb (making the kiss imagined at some point in the future) it removes the need for Iachimo to actually kiss Imogen here and now

RCT 2
Ff set a period, as if Iachimo is struck dumb by the sight of her even with her eyes closed, with the new sentence wanting even more: most modern texts reset the period as a comma, thus reducing the moment and the need

SD 3
most modern texts explain that Iachimo is removing Posthumus' bracelet from Imogen's arm

I have enough,

60   To'th'Truncke againe, and shut the spring of it.

Swift, swift, you Dragons of the night, that dawning
May beare[1] the Ravens eye: I lodge in feare,
Though this a heavenly Angell: hell is heere.

[Clocke strikes]

One, two, three: time, time.

[Exit] [2]

R 376 - e : 2.2.47 - 2.2.51

w [1]Ff = 'beare', (i.e. to 'bring'), most modern texts = 'bare' (i.e. to reveal)
sd [2] most modern texts, following the action of the speech, suggest he doesn't exit but gets back into the trunk

Scena Tertia

ENTER CLOTTEN, AND LORDS

1st. Lord	Your Lordship is the most patient man in losse, the most coldest that ever turn'd up Ace.
Cloten	It would make any man cold to loose.

1st. Lord   But not every man patient after the noble temper
of your Lordship; You are most hot, and furious when
you winne.

R 376 - e

{Cloten} [1]   Winning will put any man into courage: if I could get
this foolish Imogen, I should have Gold enough: it's al-
most morning, is't not?

1st. Lord   Day, my Lord.

Cloten   I would this Musicke would come: I am advi-
sed to give her Musicke a mornings, they say it will penetrate.

[Enter Musitians]

Come on, tune: If you can penetrate her with your fin-
gering, so: wee'l try with tongue too: if none will do, let
her remaine: but Ile never give o're.
           First, a very excel-
lent good conceyted thing; after a wonderful sweet aire,
with admirable rich words to it, and then let her consider.

SONG [2]

R 376 - e / L 377 - b   :   2.3.1 - 2.3.19

[P] [1] though the connecting mark at the bottom of F1 column R376 reminded the compositor that the next
page should start with a speech belonging to 'Clot' (i.e. Cloten), the speech prefix to start the top of L377
was not assigned: all modern texts rightfully have made the emendation as shown here

[PBS] [2] Ff do not assign a character to sing this song: thus it could be any of the musicians (who are only
referred to in the text with respect to their instrumental ability) or even Cloten himself, certainly the
unassigned speech following is his: also the words of the contemporary song differ somewhat from what
appears here: see A Textual Companion (op. cit.), page 605, note re. lines 2.3.19 - 25/868 - 74

> Hearke, hearke, the Larke at heavens gate sings
> and Phœbus gins arise,
> His Steeds to water at those Springs
> on chalic'd Flowres that lyes:
> And winking Mary-buds begin to ope their Golden eyes[1]
> With every thing that pretty is, my Lady sweet arise:
> Arise, arise.

{Cloten} [2] So, get you gone: if this penetrate,[†3] I will consider your
Musicke the better: if it do not, it is a voyce[4] in her eares
which Horse-haires, and Calves-guts, nor the voyce of
unpaved Eunuch to boot, can never amend.[†5]

ENTER CYMBALINE, AND QUEENE

2nd. Lord Heere comes the King.

Cloten I am glad I was up so late, for that's the reason
I was up so earely: he cannot choose but take this Service I have done, fatherly.
          Good morrow to your Ma-
jesty, and to my gracious Mother.

Cymbeline Attend you here the doore of our stern daughter[6]
Will she not forth?

Cloten I have assayl'd her with Musickes, but she vouch-
safes no notice.

Cymbeline The Exile of her Minion is too new,
She hath not yet forgot him, some more time
Must weare the print of his remembrance on't,[7]
And then she's yours.

Queene You are most bound to'th'King,
Who let's go by no vantages, that may
Preferre you to his daughter: Frame your selfe

[PCT] [1] Ff set no punctuation as if the passion of the song were continuing unchecked: most modern texts
add a period

[P] [2] since Ff did not assign the song to anyone (except possibly Cloten by omission) the previous speaker is
assumed to continue speaking: certainly the style and content are reminiscent of Cloten

[W] [3] F2 and most modern texts = 'penetrate', F1 = 'pen trate'

[W] [4] Ff = 'voyce', most modern texts = 'vice'

[W] [5] F2 and most modern texts = 'amend', F1 = 'amed'

[PCT] [6] F1-2 set no punctuation as if Cymbeline's sense of urgency takes over: F3/most modern texts
add a period

[W] [7] F1 = 'on't', F2 and most modern texts = 'out'

		To orderly solicity,[1] and be friended
50		With aptnesse of the season: make denials
		Encrease your Services: so seeme, as if
		You were inspir'd to do those duties which
		You tender to her: that you in all obey her,
		Save when command to your dismission tends,
55		And therein you are senselesse.

Cloten   Senselesse?
                                   Not so.

Messenger So like you (Sir) Ambassadors from Rome;
               The one is Caius Lucius.

60	**Cymbeline**	A worthy Fellow,
		Albeit he comes on angry purpose now;
		But that's no fault of his: we must receyve him
		According to the Honor of his Sender,
		And towards himselfe, his goodnesse fore-spent on us
65		We must extend our notice: Our deere Sonne,
		When you have given good morning to your Mistris,
		Attend the Queene, and us, we shall have neede
		T'employ you towards this Romane. → [2]

               Come our Queene.

[Exeunt]

70	**Cloten**	If she be up, Ile speake with her: if not
		Let her lye still, and dreame: by your leave hoa,
		I know her women are about her: what L 377 - b
		If I do line one of their hands, 'tis Gold
		Which buyes admittance (oft it doth) yea, and makes
75		Diana's Rangers false themselves, yeeld up
		Their Deere to'th'stand o'th'Stealer: and 'tis Gold
		Which makes the True-man kill'd, and saves the Theefe:
		Nay, sometime hangs both Theefe, and True-man: what
		Can it not do, and undoo?
80		I will make
		One of her women Lawyer to me, for
		I yet not understand the case my selfe.

               By your leave.
[Knockes]

[w][1] F1 = 'solicity', F2 and most modern texts = 'solicits'

[sp][2] arguing white space at the bottom of the page, most modern texts print these two short Ff lines as
one complete line: in so doing they may remove a momentary reaction from Cloten or from the Queene
sufficient to warrant Cymbeline's requesting her formally to join in leaving with him

ENTER A LADY [1]

Lady	Who's there that knockes?
Cloten	A Gentleman.
Lady	No more.
Cloten	Yes, and a Gentlewomans Sonne.
Lady	That's more Then some whose Taylors are as deere as yours, Can justly boast of: what's your Lordships pleasure?

85

90

Cloten	Your Ladies person, is she ready?
Lady	I,° to keepe her Chamber.
Cloten	There is Gold for you,° [2]

Sell me your good report.

Lady	How, my good name? or to report of you What I shall thinke is good.

95

The Princesse.

ENTER IMOGEN [3]

Cloten	Good morrow fairest, Sister your sweet hand.
Imogen	Good morrow Sir, you lay out too much paines For purchasing but trouble: the thankes I give, Is telling you that I am poore of thankes, And scarse can spare them.
Cloten	Still I sweare I love you.
Imogen	If you but said so, 'twere as deepe with me: If you sweare still, your recompence is still That I regard it not.
Cloten	This is no answer.

100

105

R 377 - b : 2.3.77 - 2.3.93

[P][1] this could be either (most probably) Helene (Imogen's Lady), the Queene's Lady, or a new character Dorothy (the character referred to later in this scene by Imogen to Pisanio)

[LS][2] this is as set in both Ff: as the symbol ° shows, most modern editions reduce the three irregular Ff lines (9/6/5 syllables) to two metric lines (10/10): however, there is the possibility for lovely interplay between the two characters, ranging from loyalty on the part of the Lady (if it is Helene or someone similarly disposed) to greed, cupidity and bribery (if not)

[SD][3] most modern texts suggest the Lady now exits: as Ff do not give her an exit anywhere it might be more interesting to see where and at whose urging she decides to leave; (from later lines where Imogen calls for Pisanio it is probable that the Lady does not stay on-stage for the whole scene)

Imogen	But that you shall not say, I yeeld being silent,
	I would not speake.
110	I pray you spare me, 'faith
	I shall unfold equall discourtesie
	To your best kindnesse: [†1] one of your great knowing
	Should learne (being taught) forbearance.
Cloten	To leave you in your madnesse, 'twere my sin,
115	I will not.
Imogen	Fooles are[2] not mad Folkes.
Cloten	Do you call me Foole?
Imogen	As I am mad, I do:
	If you'l be patient, Ile no more be mad,
120	That cures us both.
	I am much sorry (Sir)
	You put me to forget a Ladies manners
	By being so verball: and learne now, for all,
	That I which know my heart, do heere pronounce
125	By th'very truth of it, I care not for you,
	And am so neere the lacke of Charitie
	To accuse my selfe, I hate you: which I had rather
	You felt, then make't my boast.
Cloten	You sinne against
130	Obedience, which you owe your Father, for
	The Contract you pretend with that base Wretch,
	One, bred of Almes, and foster'd with cold dishes,
	With scraps o'th'Court: It is no Contract, none;
	And though it be allowed in meaner parties
135	(Yet who then he more meane) to knit their soules
	(On whom there is no more dependancie
	But Brats and Beggery) in selfe-figur'd knot,
	Yet you are curb'd from that enlargement, by
	The consequence o'th'Crowne, and must not,[3] foyle
140	The precious note of it; with a base Slave,
	A Hilding for a Livorie, a Squires Cloth,
	A Pantler; not so eminent.
Imogen	Prophane Fellow:

R 377 - b

R 377 - b / L 378 - e : 2.3.94 - 2.3.124

[W1] F2 and most modern texts = 'kindnesse', F1 = 'kinduesse'

[W2] Ff = 'are': some modern texts make the interesting gloss 'cure'

[PCT3] F1 sets a blur which could be a comma: F2/most modern texts omit the punctuation

145		Wert thou the Sonne of Jupiter, and no more,
		But what thou art besides: thou wer't too base,
		To be his Groome: thou wer't dignified enough
		Even to the point of Envie. [1]

                                If 'twere made
Comparative for your Vertues, to be stil'd
150   The under Hangman of his Kingdome; and hated
For being prefer'd so well.

Cloten   The South-Fog rot him.

Imogen   He never can meete more mischance, then come
To be but nam'd of thee.
155   His mean'st Garment
That ever hath but clipt his body; is dearer
In my respect, then all the Heires above thee,
Were they all made such men: How now Pisanio ?

                 ENTER PISANIO,[2]

Cloten   His Garments? [3]
160   Now the divell.

Imogen   To Dorothy[4] my woman hie thee presently.

Cloten   His Garment?

Imogen   I am sprighted with a Foole,
Frighted, and angred worse: Go bid my woman
165   Search for a Jewell, that too casually
Hath left mine Arme: it was thy Masters.
                            Shrew me
If I would loose it for a Revenew,
Of any Kings in Europe.
170   I do think,
I saw't this morning: Confident I am. [5]

[PCT] [1] F1 shows a period as if Imogen is overcome with her emotion and must control herself before

[SD] [2] continuing: F2/most modern texts set a comma
  usually the scripts in this series do not print the punctuation following a stage direction for it is nearly
  always a period: here, F1 shows a comma while F2 and modern texts print the usual period: this may
  be fanciful to suggest but, in Act One Scene 7, Imogen had to call for Pisanio several times to no avail
  and now he appears immediately: perhaps the comma is significant in indicating the speed of his response

[W] [3] since Imogen refers to Posthumus' 'mean'st Garment' (line 156), F2 and most modern texts amend
  F1's plural 'garments' to the single 'Garment'

[P] [4] remember that her attendant in the bedroom (Act Two Scene 2) was called Helene: this new character
  may have been the Lady we saw earlier in this scene talking to Cloten

[PCT] [5] F1-3 set a period, as if Imogen is working hard mentally and/or emotionally to deal with the situation:
  F4 reduces this to a comma, while most modern texts set major punctuation

		Last night 'twas on mine Arme; I kiss'd it,
		I hope it be not gone, to tell my Lord
		That I kisse aught but he.
		}
175	**Pisanio**	'Twill not be lost.
	Imogen	I hope so: go and search. [1]
		}
	Cloten	You have abus'd me:
		His meanest Garment?
		}
	Imogen	I, I said so Sir,
180		If you will make't an Action, call witnesse to't.
	Cloten	I will enforme your Father.
		}
	Imogen	Your Mother too:
		She's my good Lady; and will conceive, I hope
		But the worst of me.
185		So I leave your[2] Sir,
		To'th'worst of discontent.

[Exit]

	Cloten	Ile be†[3] reveng'd:
		His mean'st Garment?
		Well.

[Exit]

L 378 - e :   2.3.146 - 2.3.156

SD [1] most modern texts give an exit to Pisanio here

WD [2] F1-2 = 'your', F3 and most modern texts = 'you'

A [3] Ff print this as one, viz. 'bereveng'd', while most modern texts separate the two words and set 'be reveng'd': if the layout of Ff is accidental, as most scholars argue, then it is a delightful piece of serendipity as Cloten voices (presumably almost uncontrollably) the first inklings of what would prove horrific if his plans for revenge were to succeed later in the play

Scena Quarta

ENTER POSTHUMUS, AND PHILARIO

Posthumus	Feare it not Sir: I would I were so sure
	To winne the King, as I am bold, her Honour
	Will remaine her's.
Philario	What meanes do you make to him?
5	**Posthumus**	Not any: but abide the change of Time,
	Quake in the present winters state, and wish
	That warmer dayes would come: In these fear'd [1] hope [2]
	I barely gratifie your love; they fayling
	I must die much your debtor.
10	**Philario**	Your very goodnesse, and your company,
	Ore-payes all I can do.
	By this your King,
	Hath heard of Great Augustus: Caius Lucius,
	Will do's Commission throughly.
15		And I think
	Hee'le grant the Tribute: send th'Arrerages,
	Or looke upon our Romaines, whose remembrance
	Is yet fresh in their griefe.
Posthumus	I do beleeve
20		(Statist though I am none, nor like to be)
	That this will prove a Warre; and you shall heare
	The Legion [3] now in Gallia, sooner landed
	In our not-fearing-Britaine, then have tydings
	Of any penny Tribute paid.
25		Our Countrymen
	Are men more order'd, then when Julius Caesar
	Smil'd at their lacke of skill, but found their courage
	Worthy his frowning at.
	Their discipline,

L 378 - e

[w] [1] Ff = 'fear'd', some modern texts = 'sear'd'

[w] [2] F1 = 'hope', F2 and most modern texts = 'hopes'

[w] [3] Ff = 'Legion', some modern texts = 'Legions'

30   (Now wing-led[1] with their courages[2]) will make knowne
To their Approvers, they are People, such
That mend upon the world.

ENTER IACHIMO

Philario	See Iachimo.

Posthumus   The swiftest Harts, have posted you by land;
35   And Windes of all the Corners kiss'd your Sailes,
To make your vessell nimble.
                                    }

Philario   Welcome Sir.

Posthumus   I hope the briefenesse of your answere, made
The speedinesse of your returne.
                               }

40   **Iachimo**   Your Lady,
Is one of the fayrest that I have look'd upon[3]

Posthumus   And therewithall the best, or let her beauty
Looke thorough[4] a Casement to allure false hearts,
And be false with them.
                      }

45   **Iachimo**   Heere are Letters for you.

Posthumus   Their tenure good I trust.
                            }

Iachimo   'Tis very like.

Posthumus   Was Caius Lucius in the Britaine Court,
When you were there?
                  }

50   **Iachimo**   He was expected then,
But not approach'd.
                 }

Posthumus   All is well yet,
Sparkles this Stone as it was wont, or is't not
Too dull for your good wearing?
                         }

55   **Iachimo**   If I have[5] lost it,
I should have lost the worth of it in Gold,

[W] [1] F1 = 'wing-led', F2 = 'mingled', some modern texts = 'winged'

[W] [2] Ff = 'courages', most modern texts = 'courage'

[PCT] [3] Ff show no punctuation here, almost as if Posthumus interrupts Iachimo with his next speech: all modern texts add the final period

[W] [4] if 'thorough' is spoken as two syllables, Ff have set an eleven syllable line: some modern texts remove this possibility by setting 'through'

[W] [5] Ff = 'have', some modern texts = 'had'

Ile make a journey twice as farre, t'enjoy
A second night of such sweet shortnesse, which
Was mine in Britaine, for the Ring is wonne.

60 **Posthumus**   The Stones too hard to come by.
}

Iachimo   Not a whit,
Your Lady being so easy.
}

Posthumus   Make note[1] Sir
Your losse your Sport: I hope you know that we
65   Must not continue Friends.
}

Iachimo   Good Sir, we must
If you keepe Covenant: had I not brought
The knowledge of your Mistris home, I grant
We were to question farther; but I now
70   Professe my selfe the winner of her Honor,
Together with your Ring; and not the wronger
Of her, or you having proceeded but
By both your willes.
}

Posthumus   If you can mak't apparant
75   That you[†2] have tasted her in Bed; my hand,
And Ring is yours.
                  If not, the foule opinion
You had of her pure Honour; gaines, or looses,
Your Sword, or mine, or Masterlesse leave[3] both
80   To who shall finde them.
}

Iachimo   Sir, my Circumstances
Being so nere the Truth, as I will make them,
Must first induce you to beleeve; whose strength
I will confirme with[†4] oath, which I doubt not
85   You'l give me leave to spare, when you shall finde
You neede it not.
}

Posthumus   Proceed.
}

Iachimo   First, her Bed-chamber
(Where I confesse I slept not, but professe
90   Had that was well worth watching) it was hang'd
With Tapistry of Silke, and Silver, the Story
Proud Cleopatra, when she met her Roman,

R 378 - e

R 378 - e / L 389* - b : 2.4.43 - 2.4.70

[w][1] F1 = 'note', F2 and most modern texts = 'not'

[w][2] F2 and most modern texts = 'you', F1 = 'yon'

[w][3] Ff = 'leave' most modern texts = 'leaves'

[w][4] F1 = 'Iwill confirme wit h oath', F2 = 'I will confirme with oath'

And Sidnus swell'd above the Bankes, or for
The presse of Boates, or Pride.
95   A peece of Worke
So bravely done, so rich, that it did strive
In Workemanship, and Value, which I wonder'd
Could be so rarely, and exactly wrought
Since[1] the true life on't was ———
                                                            }

100   **Posthumus**   This is true:
And this you might have heard of heere, by me,
Or by some other.
                                                }

Iachimo   More particulars
Must justifie my knowledge.
                                                }

105   **Posthumus**   So they must,
Or doe your Honour injury.
                                                }

Iachimo   The Chimney
Is South the Chamber, and the Chimney-peece
Chaste Dian, bathing: never saw I figures
110   So likely to report themselves; the Cutter
Was as another Nature dumbe, out-went her,
Motion, and Breath left out.
                                                }

Posthumus   This is a thing
Which you might from Relation likewise reape,
115   Being, as it is, much spoke of.
                                                }

Iachimo   The Roofe o'th'Chamber,
With golden Cherubins is fretted.
                                                            Her Andirons
(I had forgot them) were two winking Cupids
120   Of Silver, each on one foote standing, nicely
Depending on their Brands.
                                                }

Posthumus   This is her Honor:
Let it be granted you have seene all this (and praise
Be given to your remembrance) the description
125   Of what is in her Chamber, nothing saves
The wager you have laid.
                                                }

Iachimo   Then if you can[2]
Be pale, I begge but leave to ayre this Jewell: See,
And now 'tis up againe: it must be married
130   To that your Diamond, Ile keepe them.

[W] [1] Ff = 'Since', most modern texts = 'Such'

[SD] [2] most modern texts suggest Iachimo now shows the bracelet he stole from Imogen

Posthumus	Jove ———— ⟩
	Once more let me behold it : Is it that
	Which I left with her?
Iachimo	Sir (I thanke her) that [1] ⟩
135		She stript it from her Arme : I see her yet :
	Her pretty Action, did out-sell her guift,
	And yet enrich'd it too : she gave it me,
	And said, she priz'd it once.
Posthumus	May be, she pluck'd it off ⟩
140		To send it me.
Iachimo	She writes so to you? doth shee? ⟩
Posthumus	O no, no, no, 'tis true.
	Heere, take this too,[2]
	It is a Basiliske unto mine eye,
145		Killes me to looke on't : Let there be no Honor,
	Where there is Beauty : Truth, where semblance : Love,
	Where there's another man.
	The Vowes of Women,
	Of no more bondage be, to where they are made,
150		Then they are to their Vertues, which is nothing :
	O, above measure false. ⟩
Philario	Have patience Sir,
	And take your Ring againe, 'tis not yet wonne :
	It may be probable she lost it : or
155		Who knowes if one her women,[4] being corrupted
	Hath stolne it from her. ⟩
Posthumus	Very true,
	And so I hope he came by't : backe my Ring,
	Render to me some corporall signe about her
160		More evident then this : for this was stolne.
Iachimo	By Jupiter, I had it from her Arme.
Posthumus	Hearke you, he sweares : by Jupiter he sweares.
	'Tis true, nay keepe the Ring ; 'tis true : I am sure

L 389[3] - b

PCT [1] Ff set no punctuation as if Iachimo's (lying) sense of joy allows to run on unbridled at the supposed memory of how Imogen removed the bracelet : most modern texts stop the flow by adding a period

SD [2] here most modern texts suggest Posthumus hands over the ring, given to him by Imogen, to Iachimo

COMP [3] the page numbers of F1 are now out of sequence : logically this should be page 379, not 389 as printed

W [4] Ff = 'one her women' : for grammatical correctness modern texts offer either 'one of her women' - thus overextending the line even more - or 'one her woman'

165		She would not loose it: her Attendants are
		All sworne, and honourable: they induc'd to steale it?
		And by a Stranger?
		No, he hath enjoy'd her,
		The Cognisance of her incontinencie
		Is this: she hath bought the name of Whore, thus deerly[1]
170		There, take thy hyre, and all the Fiends of Hell
		Divide themselves betweene you.

}

Philario	Sir, be patient:
	This is not strong enough to be beleev'd
	Of one perswaded well of.

}

175	**Posthumus**	Never talke on't:
		She hath bin colted by him.

}

Iachimo	If you seeke
	For further satisfying, under her Breast
	(Worthy her[2] pressing) lyes a Mole, right proud
180		Of that most delicate Lodging.
		By my life
		I kist it, and it gave me present hunger
		To feede againe, though full.
		You do remember
185		This staine upon her?

}

Posthumus	I, and it doth confirme
	Another staine, as bigge as Hell can hold,

	Were there no more but it.
Iachimo	Will you heare more?
190 **Posthumus**	Spare your Arethmaticke,[3]
	Never count the Turnes: ° Once, and a Million.
Iachimo	Ile be sworne.
Posthumus	No swearing: °

PCT [1] F1-2 set no punctuation as if Posthumus rushes on to give Iachimo his reward: F3/most modern texts
set up a much greater sense of self-control than first existed by adding a period at the end of the line

W [2] Ff = 'her', some modern texts = 'the'

LS [3] in Ff the actor has choice as to which two of these three short lines may be joined as one line of split
verse: however, the modern texts, regularising the third short line plus the three following (as shown by the
symbol °), have rendered poetically normal what should be the dramatic highpoint of the scene, Posthumus'
appalled revulsion and the attempt of Iachimo to finalise the lie by offering to swear it to be true: the Ff
irregularity of 3 short lines ('Were' + 'Will' + 'Spare') plus the normal 'Never' plus 2 more short lines ('Ile' + 'No')
speaks volumes in the brief silences between the highly charged words

	If you will sweare you have not done't, you lye,
195	And I will kill thee, if thou do'st deny
	Thou'st made me Cuckold.

}

Iachimo   Ile deny nothing.

Posthumus   O that I had her heere, to teare her Limb-meale:

                I will go there and doo't, i'th'Court, before

200   Her Father.

                      Ile do something.

                        [Exit]

Philario   Quite besides

                The government of Patience.

                            You have wonne:

205   Let's follow him,[1] and pervert the present wrath

                He hath against himselfe.

                    }

Iachimo   With all my heart.

                        [Exeunt]

                   ENTER POSTHUMUS

    [Most modern texts add a new scene here, Act Two, Scene 5]

Posthumus   Is there no way for Men to be, but Women

                Must be halfe-workers?

210   We are all Bastards,[2]

                And that most venerable man, which I

                Did call my Father, was, I know not where

                When I was stampt.

                        Some Coyner with his Tooles

215   Made me a counterfeit: yet my Mother seem'd

                The Dian of that time: so doth my Wife

                The Non-pareill of this.

                      Oh Vengeance, Vengeance!

                Me of my lawfull pleasure she restrain'd,

220   And pray'd me oft forbearance: did it with

                A pudencie so Rosie, the sweet view on't

                Might well have warm'd olde Saturne;

                That I thought her →[3]

                As Chaste, as un-Sunn'd Snow.

R 389* - b : 2.4.144 - 2.5.13

W[1] some modern texts remove Ff's 'him' thus reducing the 11 syllable line to pentameter

W[2] Ff = 'all Bastards', some modern texts = 'Bastards all'

LS[3] Ff offer two short lines as if the emotions momentarily get the better of Posthumus and he needs the break to get some sense of self-control: most modern texts join the two lines together

225   Oh, all the Divels!

This yellow Iachimo in an houre, was't not?   R 389 - b

Or lesse; at first?

                    Perchance he spoke not, but

Like a full Acorn'd Boare, a Iarmen on,[1]

230   Cry'de oh, and mounted; found no opposition

But what he look'd for, should oppose, and she

Should from encounter guard.

                        Could I finde out

The Womans part in me, for there's no motion

235   That tends to vice in man, but I affirme

It is the Womans part: be it Lying, note it,

The womans: Flattering, hers; Deceiving, hers:

Lust, and ranke thoughts, hers, hers: Revenges hers:

Ambitions, Covetings, change of Prides, Disdaine,

240   Nice-longing, Slanders, Mutability;

> All Faults that name,[2] nay, that Hell knowes,
>
> Why hers, in part, or all: but rather all° For even to Vice° [3]

They are not constant, but are changing still;

One Vice, but of a minute old, for one

245   Not halfe so old as that.

                    Ile write against them,

Detest them, curse them: yet 'tis greater Skill

In a true Hate, to pray they have their will:

The very Divels cannot plague them better.

[Exit]

W [1] Ff = 'Iarmen on', most modern texts = 'German one'

ALT/W [2] because this reads only as a four foot, eight syllable line in F1, various revisions have been offered, including additional words at this point of the text

        a) F1 = 'that name'

        b) F2 = 'may be nam'd'

        c) some modern texts = 'man can'

        d) other modern texts = 'man may'

LS [3] because of the irregularity of these lines various relineations have been offered: the most popular is shown with the symbol °, though some texts add 'All Faults' from the start of the first line to the end of the previous one (above the box) and do not make the emendations shown in footnote #2

Actus Tertius. Scena Prima

ENTER IN STATE, CYMBELINE, QUEENE, CLOTTEN, AND LORDS AT ONE DOORE, AND AT ANOTHER, CAIUS,[1] LUCIUS, AND ATTENDANTS

Cymbeline	Now say, what would Augustus Cæsar with us?
Lucius	When Julius Cæsar (whose remembrance yet
	Lives in mens eyes, and will to Eares and Tongues
	Be Theame, and hearing ever) was in this Britain,
	And Conquer'd it, Cassibulan[2] thine Unkle
	(Famous in Cæsars prayses, no whit lesse
	Then in his Feats deserving it) for him,
	And his Succession, granted Rome a Tribute,
	Yeerely three thousand pounds; which (by thee) lately
	Is left untender'd.

5

10

Queene	And to kill the mervaile, Shall be so ever.
Cloten	There[3] be many Cæsars, Ere such another Julius : Britaine's a world By it selfe, and we will nothing pay For wearing our owne Noses.

15

Queene	That opportunity[4] Which then they had to take from's, to resume We have againe.
	Remember Sir, my Liege, The Kings your Ancestors, together with The naturall bravery of your Isle, which stands As Neptunes Parke, ribb'd, and pal'd in

20

L 380 - b : 3.1.1 - 3.1.19

[1] since only one character is indicated in the ensuing dialogue most modern texts remove the Ff comma between 'Caius' and 'Lucius' and assign the one character both names

[2] throughout this scene F1 = 'Cassibulan', F2 and most modern texts = 'Cassibelan': this is the only time in the scene this footnoted will be offered

[3] Ff = 'There', some modern texts, because of the conditional 'Ere' starting the next line, alter this to 'Will' or 'There'll'

[4] most modern texts add this to the previous short line to create one overly long split verse line (of thirteen syllables with six strong beats): this is just as valid as the Ff pause before she attacks

		With Oakes[1] unskaleable, and roaring Waters,
25		With Sands that will not beare your Enemies Boates,
		But sucke them up to'th'Top-mast.

                          A kinde of Conquest
Cæsar made heere, but made not heere his bragge
Of Came, and Saw, and Over-came: with shame

30   (The first that ever touch'd him) he was carried
From off our Coast, twice beaten: and his Shipping
(Poore ignorant Baubles) on our terrible Seas
Like Egge-shels mov'd upon their Surges, crack'd
As easily 'gainst our Rockes.

35   For joy whereof,
The fam'd Cassibulan, who was once at point
(Oh giglet Fortune) to master Cæsars Sword,
Made Luds-Towne with rejoycing-Fires bright,   L 380 - b
And Britaines strut with Courage.

40 Cloten   Come, there's no more Tribute to be paid: our
Kingdome is stronger then it was at that time: and (as I
said) there is no mo such Cæsars , other of them may have
crook'd Noses, but to owe such straite Armes, none.

Cymbeline   Son, let your Mother end.

45 Cloten   We have yet many among us, can gripe as hard
as Cassibulan, I doe not say I am one: but I have a hand.

       Why Tribute?
                   Why should we pay Tribute?
                                 If Cæsar

50   can hide the Sun from us with a Blanket, or put the Moon
in his pocket, we will pay him Tribute for light: else Sir,
no more Tribute, pray you now.

Cymbeline   You must know,
Till the injurious Romans, did extort

55   This Tribute from us, we were free.

                              Cæsars Ambition,
Which swell'd so much, that it did almost stretch
The sides o'th'World, against all colour heere,
Did put the yoake upon's; which to shake off

60   Becomes a warlike people, whom we reckon
Our selves to be, we do. [2]

                        Say then to Cæsar,

L 380 - b / R 380 - b : 3.1.20 - 3.1.53

[W1] Ff = 'Oakes', most modern texts = 'banks' or 'rocks' (so as to maintain the watery boundary image)

[W2] Ff = ', we do.', most modern texts put a period before this phrase and either let Cymbeline start a new
sentence 'We do say to . . .' or reassign the phrase as a two word sentence 'We do.' to 'All' the English

	Our Ancestor was that Mulmutius, which
	Ordain'd our Lawes, whose use the Sword of Cæsar
65	Hath too much mangled; whose repayre, and franchise,
	Shall (by the power we hold) be our good deed,
	Tho Rome be therfore angry.

                                      Mulmutius made our lawes
Who was the first of Britaine, which did put
70   His browes within a golden Crowne, and call'd
Himselfe a King.

Lucius   I am sorry Cymbeline,
That I am to pronounce Augustus Cæsar
(Cæsar, that hath moe Kings his Servants, then
75   Thy selfe Domesticke Officers) thine Enemy:
Receyve it from me then.

                             Warre, and Confusion
In Cæsars name pronounce I 'gainst thee: Looke
For fury, not to be resisted.
80   Thus defide,
I thanke thee for my selfe.

Cymbeline   Thou art welcome Caius,
Thy Cæsar Knighted me; my youth I spent
Much under him: of him, I gather'd Honour,
85   Which he, to seeke of me againe, perforce,
Behooves me keepe at utterance.

                                I am perfect,
That the Pannonians and Dalmatians, for
Their Liberties are now in Armes: a President
90   Which not to reade, would shew the Britaines cold:
So Cæsar shall not finde them.

Lucius   Let proofe speake.

Cloten   His Majesty biddes you welcome.

                                  Make pa-
95   stime with us, a day, or two, or longer: if you seek us af-
terwards in other tearmes, you shall finde us in our Salt-
water-Girdle: if you beate us out of it, it is yours: if you
fall in the adventure, our Crowes shall fare the better fore
you: and there's an end.

100 **Lucius**   So sir.

Cymbeline   I know your Masters pleasure, and he mine:
All the Remaine, is welcome.

[Exeunt]

Scena Secunda

ENTER PISANIO READING OF A LETTER

Pisanio	How? of Adultery?
	Wherefore write you not

How? of Adultery?
                 Wherefore write you not
What Monsters her accuse? [1]
                     Leonatus:
5   Oh Master, what a strange infection   R 380 - b
Is falne into thy eare?
                   What false Italian,
(As poysonous tongu'd, as handed) hath prevail'd
On thy too ready hearing?
10   Disloyall?
                       No.

She's punish'd for her Truth; and undergoes
More Goddesse-like, then Wife-like; such Assaults
As would take in some Vertue.
15   Oh my Master,
Thy mind to her, [2] is now as lowe, as were
Thy Fortunes.
            How?
                 That I should murther her,
20   Upon the Love, and Truth, and Vowes; which I
Have made to thy command?
                 I her?
                  Her blood?

If it be so, to do good service, never
25   Let me be counted serviceable.
                How looke I,
That I should seeme to lacke humanity,
So much as this Fact comes to?
                 [3] Doo't: The Letter.

R 380 - b / L 381 - e : 3.2.1 - 3.2.17

W[1] Ff = 'accuse', one modern gloss = 'accuser'

W[2] Ff = 'her', most modern texts = 'her's'

SD[3] most modern texts add a stage direction that Pisanio is now reading from the letter, and that as a consequence the words 'Doo't' and 'The Letter' are phrases within the letter (set on the next page)

30 *That I have sent her, by her owne command,*
    Shall give thee opportunitie.
                              Oh damn'd paper,
    Blacke as the Inke that's on thee : senselesse bauble,
    Art thou a Fœdarie for this Act ; and look'st
35 So Virgin-like without?
                              Loe here she comes.

ENTER IMOGEN

    I am ignorant in what I am commanded.

Imogen   How now Pisanio?

Pisanio   Madam, heere is a Letter from my Lord.

40 **Imogen**   Who, thy Lord?
                              That is my Lord Leonatus?

    Oh, learn'd indeed were that Astronomer
    That knew the Starres, as I his Characters,
    Heel'd lay the Future open.
45   You good Gods,
    Let what is heere contain'd, rellish of Love,
    Of my Lords health, of his content : yet not
    That we two are asunder, let that grieve him ;
    Some griefes are medcinable, that is one of them,
50 For it doth physicke Love, of his content,
    All but in that.
                    Good Wax, thy leave : blest be
    You Bees that make these Lockes of counsaile.
                                          Lovers,
55 And men in dangerous Bondes pray not alike,
    Though Forfeytours you cast in prison, yet
    You claspe young Cupids Tables : good Newes Gods. [1]

    Justice and your Fathers wrath (should he take me in his
    Dominion) could not be so cruell to me, as you: (oh the dee-
60 *rest of Creatures) would even renew me with your eyes.*
                                          Take
    notice that I am in Cambria at Milford-Haven: what your
    owne Love, will out of this advise you, follow.
                                  So he wishes you
65 *all happinesse, that remaines loyall to his Vow, and your encrea-*
    sing in Love .
                              Leonatus Posthumus .

L 381 - e   :   3.2.18 - 3.2.47

[SD 1] most modern texts explain that now Imogen reads the letter

Oh for a Horse with wings: Hear'st thou Pisanio?
He is at Milford-Haven: Read, and tell me
How farre 'tis thither.
                              If one of meane affaires
70 May plod it in a weeke, why may not I
Glide thither in a day?
                              Then true Pisanio ,
Who long'st like me, to see thy Lord; who long'st
75 (Oh let me bate) but not like me: yet long'st
But in a fainter kinde.
                              Oh not like me:
For mine's beyond, beyond: say, and speake thicke
(Loves Counsailor should fill the bores of hearing,
80 To'th'smothering of the Sense) how farre it is
To this same blessed Milford.
                              And by'th'way
Tell me how Wales was made so happy, as
T'inherite such a Haven.
85   But first of all,
How we may steale from hence: and for the gap
That we shall make in Time, from our hence-going,
And[1] our returne, to excuse: but first, how get hence.
Why should excuse be borne or ere begot?
90 Weele talke of that heereafter.
                              Prythee speake,
How many store[2] of Miles may we well rid[3]   L 381 - e
Twixt houre, and houre?
                                        }
Pisanio   One score 'twixt Sun, and Sun,
95 Madam's enough for you: and too much too.

Imogen   Why, one that rode to's Excution[4] Man,
Could never go so slow: I have heard of Riding wagers,
Where Horses have bin nimbler then the Sands
That run i'th'Clocks behalfe.
100   But this is Foolrie,
Go, bid my Woman faigne a Sicknesse, say
She'le home to her Father; and provide me presently
A Riding Suit: No costlier then would fit
A Franklins Huswife.

L 381 - e / R 381 - e   :   3.2.48 - 3.2.77

[w1] Ff = 'And', most modern texts = 'Till' or 'To'

[w2] Ff = 'store', most modern texts = 'score'

[w3] Ff = 'rid', most modern texts = 'ride'

[w4] F1 = 'Excution', F2 = 'Execution'

105   **Pisanio**   Madam, you're best consider.

      Imogen   I see before me (Man) nor heere, not [1] heere;
                             Nor what ensues but have a Fog in them
                             That I cannot looke through.
                                             Away, I prythee,
110   Do as I bid thee: There's no more to say:
                             Accessible is none but Milford way.

[Exeunt]

R 381 - e : 3.2.77 - 3.2.82

[W][1] F1 = 'not', F2 and most modern texts = 'nor' (while some modern texts revamp the line to 'not.......nor'):
also, the F1 semi-colon that follows allows Imogen a moment to recover from whatever emotions she has
created within herself: most modern texts follow F2 and set a comma

Scena Tertia

ENTER BELARIUS, GUIDERIUS, AND ARVIRAGUS [1] [2]

Belarius	A goodly day, not to keepe house with such,
	Whose Roofe's as lowe as ours: Sleepe[3] Boyes, this gate
	Instructs you how t'adore the Heavens; and bowes you
	To a mornings holy office.

5   The Gates of Monarches
Are Arch'd so high, that Giants may jet through
And keepe their impious Turbonds on, without
Good morrow to the Sun.
                              Haile thou faire Heaven,

10   We house i'th'Rocke, yet use thee not so hardly
As prouder livers do.

Guiderius	Haile Heaven.
Arviragus	Haile Heaven.

Belarius	Now for our Mountaine sport, up to yond hill
15	Your legges are yong: Ile tread these Flats.

                                     Consider,
When you above perceive me like a Crow,
That it is Place, which lessens, and sets off,
And you may then revolve what Tales, I have told you,
20   Of Courts, of Princes; of the Tricks in Warre.

This[4] Service is not Service; so being done,
But being so allowed.
                         To apprehend thus,
Drawes us a profit from all things we see:
25   And often to our comfort, shall we finde
The sharded-Beetle, in a safer hold
Then is the full-wing'd Eagle.
                         Oh this life,
Is Nobler, then attending for a checke:

[P][1] it is interesting to note that the two boys are named in the text as their real father Cymbeline christened them , not as Polydore and Cadwall (the aliases given them by Belarius)

[SD][2] most modern texts add that they enter from their Cave

[W][3] Ff = 'Sleepe', most modern texts emend this to 'Stoop'

[W][4] though most modern texts agree with Ff and print 'This', one interesting gloss = 'That'

30   Richer, then doing nothing for a Babe: [1]
       Prouder, then rustling in unpayd-for Silke:
       Such gaine the Cap of him, that makes him[2] fine,
       Yet keepes his Booke uncros'd: no life to ours.

Guiderius   Out of your proofe you speak: we poore unfledg'd
35   Have never wing'd from view o'th'nest; nor knowes[3] not
       What Ayre's from home.
                              Hap'ly this life is best,
       (If quiet life be best) sweeter to you
       That have a sharper knowne.
40   Well corresponding
       With your stiffe Age; but unto us, it is
       A Cell of Ignorance: travailing a bed,
       A Prison, or[4] a Debtor, that not dares
       To stride a limit.

45 **Arviragus**   What should we speake of
       When we are old as you?
                              When we shall heare
       The Raine and winde beate darke December?
                                                How
50   In this our pinching Cave, shall we discourse   R 381-e
       The freezing houres away?
                                 We have seene nothing:
       We are beastly; subtle as the Fox for prey,
       Like warlike as the Wolfe, for what we eate:
55   Our Valour is to chace what flyes: Our Cage
       We make a Quire, as doth the prison'd Bird,
       And sing our Bondage freely.

Belarius   How you speake.

       Did you but know the Citties Usuries,
60   And felt them knowingly: the Art o'th'Court,
       As hard to leave, as keepe: whose top to climbe
       Is certaine falling: or so slipp'ry, that
       The feare's as bad as falling.
                                      The toyle o'th'Warre,
65   A paine that onely seemes to seeke out danger
       I'th'name of Fame, and Honor, which dyes i'th'search,
       And hath as oft a sland'rous Epitaph,
       As Record of faire Act.

[W1] Ff = 'Babe', most modern texts = 'bable' (i.e. a bauble, a nothing)

[W2] Ff = 'him', most modern texts = "em'

[W3] F1 = 'knowes', F2 and most modern texts = 'know'

[W4] most modern texts set Ff's ', or', one gloss removes the comma changing 'or' to 'for' viz. 'A Prison for a Debtor'

		Nay, many times
70		Doth ill deserve, by doing well: what's worse
		Must curt'sie at the Censure.
		Oh Boyes, this Storie

Nay, many times
Doth ill deserve, by doing well: what's worse
Must curt'sie at the Censure.
                              Oh Boyes, this Storie
The world may reade in me: My bodie's mark'd,
With Roman Swords; and my report, was once
First, with the best of Note.
                              Cymbeline lov'd me,
And when a Souldier was the Theame, my name
Was not farre off: then was I as a Tree
Whose boughes did bend with fruit.
                              But in one night,
A Storme, or Robbery (call it what you will)
Shooke downe my mellow hangings: nay my Leaves,
And left me bare to weather. ⟩

Guiderius   Uncertaine favour.

Belarius   My fault being nothing (as I have told you oft)
But that two Villaines, whose false Oathes prevayl'd
Before my perfect Honor, swore to Cymbeline,
I was Confederate with the Romanes: so
Followed my Banishment, and this twenty yeeres,
This Rocke, and these Demesnes, have bene my World,
Where I have liv'd at honest freedome, payed
More pious debts to Heaven, then in all
The fore-end of my time.
                              But, up to'th'Mountaines,
This is not Hunters Language; he that strikes
The Venison first, shall be the Lord o'th'Feast,
To him the other two shall minister,
And we will feare no poyson, which attends
In place of greater State: →[1]
Ile meete you in the Valleyes.

[Exeunt]

How hard it is to hide the sparkes of Nature?

These Boyes know little they are Sonnes to'th'King,
Nor Cymbeline dreames that they are alive.

They thinke they are mine, →
And though train'd up thus meanely
I'th'Cave, whereon the Bowe[2] their thoughts do hit,

[SP][1] both here and in 5 lines time Ff show a split line for Belarius, as if he is overcome with his own thoughts and needs a moment to recover: each time modern texts join the lines as one

[W][2] Ff = 'whereon the Bowe', most modern texts sensibly emend this to = 'wherein they bow' plus a comma

The Roofes of Palaces, and Nature prompts them
In simple and lowe things, to Prince it, much
Beyond the tricke of others.

110   This Paladour,[1]
The heyre of Cymbeline and Britaine, who
The King his Father call'd Guiderius.
                          Jove,
When on my three-foot stoole I sit, and tell
115   The warlike feats I have done, his spirits flye out
Into my Story: say thus mine Enemy fell,
And thus I set my foote on's necke, even then
The Princely blood flowes in his Cheeke, he sweats,
Straines his yong Nerves, and puts himselfe in posture
120   That acts my words.
                    The yonger Brother Cadwall,
Once Arviragus, in as like a figure
Strikes life into my speech, and shewes much more
His owne conceyving.
125   [2] Hearke, the Game is rows'd,
Oh Cymbeline, Heaven and my Conscience knowes
Thou didd'st unjustly banish me: whereon   L 382 - b
At three, and two yeeres old, I stole these Babes,
Thinking to barre thee of Succession, as
130   Thou refts me of my Lands.
                          Euriphile,
Thou was't their Nurse, they took thee for their mother,
And every day do honor to her grave:
My selfe Belarius, that am Morgan†[3] call'd
135   They take for Naturall Father.
                    The Game is up.

[Exit]

W[1] Ff = 'Paladour', most modern texts = 'Polidour' or 'Polydore'

F[2] several scholars have problems in accepting the text from here to the end of the scene as vintage
    Shakespeare: at best they suggest it arose as a Shakespearean afterthought, at worst it is not
    Shakespearean at all: (one critic goes as far as to doubt the authenticity of the whole scene): see William
    Shakespeare: A Textual Companion, op. cit., page 607, notes re. lines 3.3.99 - 107/1454 - 1462

W[3] F1 = 'Mergan', F2 and most modern texts = 'Morgan'

Scena Quarta

ENTER PISANIO AND IMOGEN

Imogen	Thou told'st me when we came frö horse, ÿ¹ place
	Was neere at hand: Ne're long'd my Mother so
	To see me first, as I have now.
	Pisanio, Man:

Imogen
Thou told'st me when we came frö horse, ÿ¹ place
Was neere at hand: Ne're long'd my Mother so
To see me first, as I have now.
                              Pisanio, Man:
Where is Posthumus?
                              What is in thy mind
That makes thee stare thus?
                              Wherefore breaks that sigh
From th'inward of thee?
                              One, but painted thus
Would be interpreted a thing perplex'd
Beyond selfe-explication.
                              Put thy selfe
Into a haviour of lesse feare, ere wildnesse
Vanquish my stayder Senses.
                              What's the matter?²

Why tender'st thou that Paper to me, with
A looke untender?
                              If't be Summer Newes
Smile too't before: if Winterly, thou need'st
But keepe that count'nance stil.
                              My Husbands hand?
That Drug-damn'd Italy, hath out-craftied him,
And hee's at some hard point.
                              Speake man, thy Tongue
May take off some extreamitie, which to reade
Would be even mortall to me.
                              }

Pisanio
Please you reade,
And you shall finde me (wretched man) a thing
The most disdain'd of Fortune.

AB ¹ originally foreshortened due to lack of column width in Ff, most modern texts reproduce 'frö' and 'ÿ'
as 'from' and 'the'

SD ² most modern texts explain here Pisanio gives her another letter from Posthumus: they usually fail to
add that (from the dialogue) the letter is clearly not addressed to Imogen but to Pisanio, the one he was
reading in his last scene, Act Three Scene 2

IMOGEN READES

Thy [†] *Mistris (Pisanio) hath plaide the Strumpet in my*
Bed: the Testimonies whereof, lyes bleeding in me.

           I speak
35 *not out of weake Surmises, but from proofe as strong as my*
greefe, and as certaine as I expect my Revenge.

          That part, thou
(Pisanio) must acte for me, if thy Faith be not tainted with the
breach of hers; let thine owne hands take away her life: I shall
40 *give thee opportunity at Milford Haven.*

          She hath my Letter
for the purpose; where, if thou feare to strike, and to make mee
certaine it is done, thou art the Pander to her dishonour, and
equally to me disloyall.

Pisanio   What shall I need to draw my Sword, the Paper
45   Hath cut her throat alreadie?

                    No, 'tis Slander,
Whose edge is sharper then the Sword, whose tongue
Out-venomes all the Wormes of Nyle, whose breath
Rides on the posting windes, and doth belye
50   All corners of the World.

                    Kings, Queenes, and States,
Maides, Matrons, nay the Secrets of the Grave
This viperous slander enters.

                        What cheere, Madam?

55 **Imogen**   False to his Bed?

                    What is it to be false?
To lye in watch there, and to thinke on him?
To weepe 'twixt clock and clock?

                    If sleep charge Nature,
60   To breake it with a fearfull dreame of him,
And cry my selfe awake?

                That's false to's bed?

                        Is it?

Pisanio   Alas good Lady.

65 **Imogen**   I false?

             Thy Conscience witnesse: Iachimo,
Thou didd'st accuse him of Incontinencie,
Thou then look'dst like a Villaine: now, me thinkes   R 382 - b
Thy favours good enough.
70   Some Jay of Italy
(Whose mother was her painting) hath betraid him:

Poore I am stale, a Garment out of fashion,
And for I am richer then to hang by th'walles,
I must be ript: To peeces with me: Oh!

75 Mens Vowes are womens Traitors.
                        All good seeming
By thy revolt (oh Husband) shall be thought
Put on for Villainy; not borne where't growes,
But worne a Baite for Ladies.
                              }

Pisanio   80   Good Madam, heare me.

Imogen   True honest men being heard, like false Æneas,
Were in his time thought false: and Synons weeping
Did scandall many a holy teare: tooke pitty
From most true wretchednesse.
85   So thou, Posthumus
Wilt lay the Leaven on all proper men;
Goodly, and gallant, shall be false and perjur'd
From thy great faile: Come Fellow, be thou honest,
Do thou thy Masters bidding.
90   When thou seest him,
A little witnesse my obedience.
                          Looke
I draw the Sword my selfe, take it, and hit
The innocent Mansion of my Love (my Heart:)
95 Feare not, 'tis empty of all things, but Greefe:
Thy Master is not there, who was indeede
The riches of it.
                   Do his bidding, strike,
Thou mayst be valiant in a better cause;
100 But now thou seem'st a Coward.
                            }

Pisanio   Hence vile Instrument, [1]
Thou shalt not damne my hand.
                        }

Imogen   Why, I must dye:
And if I do not by thy hand, thou art
105 No Servant of thy Masters.
                         Against Selfe-slaughter,
There is a prohibition so Divine,
That cravens my weake hand: Come, heere's my heart:
Something's a-foot: [2] Soft, soft, wee'l no defence,
110 Obedient as the Scabbard.

SD 1 some modern texts add the stage direction that here Pisanio puts aside Imogen's sword

SD/W 2 most modern texts explain that in preparing herself for death she discovers (at least one) letter(s)
from Posthumus next her heart: also while Ff = 'a-foot', some modern texts = 'a-for't'

What is heere,
The Scriptures of the Loyall Leonatus,
All turn'd to Heresie?

            Away, away

115 Corrupters of my Faith, you shall no more
Be Stomachers to my heart: thus may poore Fooles
Beleeve false Teachers: Though those that are betraid
Do feele the Treason sharpely, yet the Traitor
Stands in worse case of woe.

120   And thou Posthumus,
That didd'st set up my disobedience 'gainst the King
My Father, and makes[1] me put into contempt the suites
Of Princely Fellowes, shalt heereafter finde
It is no acte of common passage, but

125 A straine of Rarenesse: and I greeve my selfe,
To thinke, when thou shalt be disedg'd by her,
That now thou tyrest on, how thy memory
Will then be pang'd by me.

                Prythee dispatch,

130 The Lambe entreats the Butcher.

                    Wher's thy knife?

Thou art too slow to do thy Masters bidding
When I desire it too.

Pisanio Oh gracious Lady:

135 Since I receiv'd command to do this businesse,
I have not slept one winke.

Imogen Doo't, and to bed then.

Pisanio Ile wake mine eye-balles[2] first.

Imogen Wherefore then
140 Didd'st undertake it?

                Why hast thou abus'd
So many Miles, with a pretence? This place?
Mine Action? and thine owne? Our Horses labour?
The Time inviting thee? The perturb'd Court
145 For my being absent? whereunto I never
Purpose returne.[3]

L 383 - b : 3.4.80 - 3.4.107

[w1] Ff = 'makes', most modern texts = 'make'

[w2] though Ff have no extra words here, some modern texts add 'out', both for meaning and rendering an imperfect split-line to metric regularity

[st3] there could be as many as six separate questions/sentences here: however, this edition shows the passage as just one rhetorical unit for the speed of action: the reader/actress is invited to choose whichever combination of between one and six sentences seems appropriate

		Why hast thou gone so farre	
		To be un-bent? when thou hast 'tane thy stand,	L 383 - e
		Th'elected Deere before thee?	

150 **Pisanio** But to win time
To loose so bad employment, in the which

I have consider'd of a course: good Ladie
Heare me with patience.

Imogen Talke thy tongue weary, speake:
155 I have heard I am a Strumpet, and mine eare
Therein false strooke, can take no greater wound,
Nor tent, to bottome that.
But speake.

Pisanio Then Madam,
160 I thought you would not backe againe.

Imogen Most like,
Bringing me heere to kill me.

Pisanio Not so neither:
But if I were as wise, as honest, then
165 My purpose would prove well: it cannot be,
But that my Master is abus'd.
Some Villaine,
I, and singular in his Art, hath done you both
This cursed injurie.

170 **Imogen** Some Roman Curtezan?

Pisanio No, on my life: [1]
Ile give but notice you are dead, and send him
Some bloody signe of it.
For 'tis commanded
175 I should do so: you shall be mist at Court,
And that will well confirme it.

Imogen Why good Fellow,
What shall I do the while?
Where bide?
How live?
180 Or in my life, what comfort, when I am
Dead to my Husband?

Pisanio If you'l backe to'th'Court.

[LS][1] the actor has choice as to which two of these three short lines may be joined as one line of split verse

Imogen		No Court, no Father, nor no more adoe
185		With that harsh, noble,[1] simple nothing:
		That Clotten, whose Love-suite hath bene to me
		As fearefull as a Siege.
		⟩
Pisanio		If not at Court,
		Then not in Britaine must you bide.
		⟩
190	**Imogen**	Where then?

Hath Britaine all the Sunne that shines?

                          Day?

                             Night?

Are they not but in Britaine?

195   I'th'worlds Volume

Our Britaine seemes as of it, but not in't:

In a great Poole, a Swannes-nest, prythee thinke

There's livers out of Britaine.

                     ⟩

Pisanio		I am most glad
200		You thinke of other place: Th'Ambassador,
		Lucius the Romane comes to Milford-Haven
		To morrow.

                    Now, if you could weare a minde

Darke, as your Fortune is, and but disguise

205 That which t'appeare it selfe, must not yet be,

But by selfe-danger, you should tread a course

Pretty, and full of view: yea, happily, neere

The residence of Posthumus; so nie (at least)

That though his Actions were not visible yet

210 Report should render him hourely to your eare,

As truely as he mooves.

                   ⟩

Imogen		Oh for such meanes,
		Though perill to my modestie, not death on't
		I would adventure.

                   ⟩

215	**Pisanio**	Well then, heere's the point:
		You must forget to be a Woman: change
		Command, into obedience.

                        Feare, and Nicenesse

(The Handmaides of all Women, or more truely

220 Woman it pretty selfe) into a waggish courage,

Ready in gybes, quicke-answer'd, sawcie and

As quarrellous as the Weazell: Nay, you must

[W][1] though most modern texts agree with Ff and print this as 'noble', one interesting gloss argues that
because of both the metric irregularity (a nine syllable line as set in Ff) and the inappropriateness of the
word 'noble', the word should be replaced with the phrase 'churlish feeble'

Forget that rarest Treasure of your Cheeke,
Exposing it (but oh the harder heart,   R 383 - b
225   Alacke no remedy) to the greedy touch
Of common-kissing Titan: and forget
Your laboursome and dainty Trimmes, wherein
You made great Juno angry.
                                        ⌡

Imogen   Nay be breefe?
230   I see into thy end, and am almost
A man already.

Pisanio   First, make your selfe but like one,   ⌡
Fore-thinking this. [1]
                    I have already fit
235   ('Tis in my Cloake-bagge) Doublet, Hat, Hose, all
That answer to them: Would you in their serving,
(And with what imitation you can borrow
From youth of such a season) 'fore Noble Lucius
Present your selfe, desire his service: tell him
240   Wherein you're happy; which will make him know,
If that his head have eare in Musicke, doubtlesse
With joy he will imbrace you: for hee's Honourable,
And doubling that, most holy.
                                        Your meanes abroad:
245   You have me rich, and I will never faile
Beginning, nor supplyment.
                                        ⌡

Imogen   Thou art all the comfort
The Gods will diet me with.
                                        Prythee away,
250   There's more to be consider'd: but wee'l even
All that good time will give us.
                                        This attempt,
I am Souldier too, and will abide it with
A Princes Courage.
                                        Away, I prythee.

255

Pisanio   Well Madam, we must take a short farewell,
Least being mist, I be suspected of
Your carriage from the Court.
                                        My Noble Mistris,
260   Heere is a boxe, I had it from the Queene,

R 383 - b / L 384 - b : 3.4.160 - 3.4.188

PCT [1]
    in this sentence, Ff's last two pieces of punctuation are a comma and then a period: most modern
    texts reverse their order: though totally incorrect grammatically, Ff is dramatically alive, allowing Pisanio
    to rush through the first daring moment and then pause (either because of Imogen's reaction or because
    he is searching for the clothes)

What's in't is precious: If you are sicke at Sea,
Or Stomacke-qualm'd at Land, a Dramme of this
Will drive away distemper.
                         To some shade,

265 And fit you to your Manhood: may the Gods
Direct you to the best.

Imogen   Amen: I thanke thee.

[Exeunt]

Scena Quinta

ENTER CYMBELINE, QUEENE, CLOTEN, LUCIUS,
AND LORDS

Cymbeline	Thus farre, and so farewell.
Lucius	Thankes, Royall Sir:
	My emperor hath wrote, I must from hence,
	And am right sorry, that I must report ye
	My Masters Enemy.
Cymbeline	Our Subjects (Sir)
	Will not endure his yoake; and for our selfe
	To shew lesse Soveraignty then they, must needs
	Appeare un-Kinglike.
Lucius	So Sir: I desire of you
	A Conduct over Land to Milford-Haven.
	Madam, all joy befall your Grace, and you.
Cymbeline	My Lords, you are appointed for that Office:
	The due of Honor, in no point omit:
	So farewell Noble Lucius.
Lucius	Your hand, my Lord.
Cloten	Receive it friendly: but from this time forth
	I weare it as your Enemy.
Lucius	Sir, the Event
	Is yet to name the winner.
	Fare you well.
Cymbeline	Leave not the worthy Lucius, good my Lords
	Till he have crost the Severn.
	Happines.

5

10

15

20

[Exit Lucius & c.]

L 384 - b

25	**Queene**	He goes hence frowning: but it honours us
		That we have given him cause.
		}
	Cloten	'Tis all the better,
		Your valiant Britaines have their wishes in it.
	Cymbeline	Lucius hath wrote already to the Emperor
30		How it goes heere.
		It fits us therefore ripely
		Our Chariots, and our Horsemen be in readinesse:
		The Powres that he already hath in Gallia
		Will soone be drawne to head, from whence he moves
35		His warre for Britaine.
		}
	Queene	'Tis not sleepy businesse,
		But must be look'd too speedily, and strongly.
	Cymbeline	Our expectation that it would be thus
		Hath made us forward.
40		But my gentle Queene,
		Where is our Daughter?
		She hath not appear'd
		Before the Roman, nor to us hath tender'd
		The duty of the day.
45		She lookes†1 us like
		A thing more made of malice, then of duty,
		We have noted it.
		Call her before us, for
		We have beene too slight in sufferance. 2
50	**Queene**	Royall Sir,3
		Since the exile of Posthumus, most retyr'd
		Hath her life bin: the Cure whereof, my Lord,
		'Tis time must do.
		Beseech your Majesty,
55		Forbeare sharpe speeches to her.
		Shee's a Lady
		So tender of rebukes, that words are strokes,†4
		And strokes death to her.

ENTER A MESSENGER

W1 F1 = 'looke', F2 and most modern texts = 'lookes'

SD2 most modern texts add a stage direction here for a Servant/Messenger to exit to return in six lines time

LS3 most modern texts join this to the previous line from Cymbeline to form one slightly lengthy split
verse line: however, with the necessary exit of the Servant, the Ff layout might serve the dramatic action
better, especially if the Queene needs to be careful in applying the next stage of her verbal poison

W4 F2 and most modern texts = 'strokes,', F1 = 'stroke;'

Cymbeline	Where is she Sir?
60	How
	Can her contempt be answer'd? }
Messenger	Please you Sir,
	Her Chambers are all lock'd, and there's no answer
	That will be given to'th'lowd [1] of noise, we make.
65 **Queene**	My Lord, when last I went to visit her,
	She pray'd me to excuse her keeping close,
	Whereto constrain'd by her infirmitie,
	She should that dutie leave unpaide to you
	Which dayly she was bound to proffer: this
70	She wish'd me to make knowne: but our great Court
	Made me too blame in memory. }
Cymbeline	Her doores lock'd?

	Not seene of late?
	Grant Heavens, that which I
75	Feare,° prove false.
	[Exit]
Queene	Sonne, I say, follow the King. ° [2]

Cloten	That man of hers, Pisanio, her old Servant
	I have not seene these two dayes.
	[Exit]
Queene	Go, looke after:
80	Pisanio, thou that stand'st so for Posthumus,
	He hath a Drugge of mine: I pray, his absence
	Proceed by swallowing that.
	For he beleeves
	It is a thing most precious.
85	But for her,
	Where is she gone?
	Haply dispaire hath seiz'd her:
	Or wing'd with fervour of her love, she's flowne
	To her desir'd Posthumus: gone she is,
90	To death, or to dishonor, and my end
	Can make good use of either.

[W 1] Ff = 'lowd' most modern texts = 'loud'st' or 'loudest'

[LS 2] this is as set in Ff: however, as the symbol ° shows, most modern editions reduce the three irregular
Ff lines (9/3/7 syllables respectively) to two rhythmically irregular lines of 10/9 syllables: this condenses
and regularises far too neatly the blazing abruptness of the reactions of both Cymbeline and then the
Queene to the news: the irregularity of Ff allows for both silence plus thought, and for action

Shee being downe,
I have the placing of the Brittish Crowne.

ENTER CLOTEN

How now, my Sonne?

95	**Cloten**	'Tis certaine she is fled: ⎫ Go in and cheere the King, he rages, none Dare come about him. ⎫
	Queene	All the better: may This night fore-stall him of the comming day. [1]

[Exit Queene]

100	**Cloten**	I love, and hate her: for she's Faire and Royall,
		And that she hath all courtly parts more exquisite R 384 - b
		Then Lady, Ladies, Woman, from every one
		The best she hath, and shee of all compounded
		Out-selles them all.
105		I love her therefore, but
		Disdaining me, and throwing Favours on
		The low Posthumus, slanders so her judgement,
		That what's else rare, is choak'd: and in that point
		I will conclude to hate her, nay indeede,
110		To be reveng'd upon her.
		For, when Fooles shall —— [2]

ENTER PISANIO

Who is heere?

		What, are you packing sirrah?
		Come hither: Ah you precious Pandar, Villaine,
115		Where is thy Lady?
		In a word, or else
		Thou art straightway with the Fiends. ⎫
	Pisanio	Oh, good my Lord.
	Cloten	Where is thy Lady?
120		Or, by Jupiter,
		I will not aske againe.

[A]1 most modern texts indicate this is spoken as an aside: if so, this presumes the Queene has not informed Cloten of her plot to get rid of Cymbeline

[LS]2 Ff set an eleven syllable line, as if Cloten's emotions are getting the better of him (and who knows where he might finish up if not interrupted): peculiarly, some modern texts remove Ff's 'shall' from the end of this line and add it to the start of the next (creating an eleven syllable line where pentameter existed before), thus reducing the Ff imbalance that originally existed

Close Villaine,
Ile have this Secret from thy heart,[1] or rip
Thy heart to finde it.

125   Is she with Posthumus?
From whose so many waights of basenesse, cannot
A dram of worth be drawne.

Pisanio   Alas, my Lord,
How can she be with him?

130   When was she miss'd?

He is in Rome.

Cloten   Where is she Sir?
               Come neerer:
No farther halting: satisfie me home,

135   What is become of her?

Pisanio   Oh, my all-worthy Lord.

Cloten   All-worthy Villaine,[2]

Discover where thy Mistris is, at once,
At the next word: no more of worthy Lord:

140 Speake, or thy silence on the instant, is
Thy condemnation, and thy death.

Pisanio   Then Sir:
This Paper is the historie of my knowledge
Touching her flight.

145 **Cloten**   Let's see't:[3] I will pursue her
Even to Augustus Throne.

Pisanio   Or this, or perish.[4]

She's farre enough, and what he learnes by this,
May prove his travell, not her danger.

150 **Cloten**   Humh.

Pisanio   Ile write to my Lord she's dead: Oh Imogen,
Safe mayst thou wander, safe returne agen.[5]

Cloten   Sirra, is this Letter true?

L 385 - b : 3.5.86 - 3.5.106

[W 1] though some modern texts agree with Ff and print this as 'heart', several texts dislike the heart/heart
image and alter the first 'heart' to 'mouth' or 'lips' or 'tongue'

[SP 2] the actor has choice as to which two of these three short lines may be joined as one line of split verse

[SD 3] most modern texts explain that Pisanio gives Cloten the first (friendly) letter from Posthumus

[A 4] most modern texts indicate this is spoken as an aside

[A 5] ditto

	Pisanio	Sir, as I thinke.
155	**Cloten**	It is Posthumus hand, I know't.

Sirrah, if thou
would'st not be a Villain, but do me true service: under-
go those Imployments wherin I should have cause to use
thee with a serious industry, that is, what villainy soere I
160   bid thee do to performe it, directly and truely, I would
thinke thee an honest man: thou should'st neither want
my meanes for thy releefe, nor my voyce for thy preferment.

    Pisanio   Well, my good Lord.

165   **Cloten**   Wilt thou serve mee?

For since patiently and
constantly thou hast stucke to the bare Fortune of that
Begger Posthumus, thou canst not in the course of grati-
tude, but be a diligent follower of mine.

170   Wilt thou serve
mee?

    Pisanio   Sir, I will.

    Cloten   Give mee thy hand, heere's my purse.

Hast any
175   of thy late Masters Garments in thy possession?

    Pisanio   I have (my Lord) at my Lodging, the same
Suite he wore, when he tooke leave of my Ladie & Mi-
stresse.

    Cloten   The first service thou dost mee, fetch that Suite   L 385 · b
180   hither, let it be thy first service, go.

    Pisanio   I shall my Lord.

[Exit]

    Cloten   Meet thee at Milford-Haven: (I forgot to aske
him one thing, Ile remember't anon:) even there, thou
villaine Posthumus will I kill thee.

185   I would these Gar-
ments were come.

She saide upon a time (the bitternesse
of it, I now belch from my heart) that shee held the very
Garment of Posthumus, in more respect, then my Noble
190   and naturall person; together with the adornement of
my Qualities.

With that Suite upon my backe wilI ra-
vish her: first kill him, and in her eyes; there shall she see
my valour, which wil then be a torment to hir contempt.

195 He on the ground, my speech of insulment [1] ended on his
dead bodie, and when my Lust hath dined (which, as I
say, to vex her, I will execute in the Cloathes that she so
prais'd:) to the Court Ile knock her backe, foot her home
againe.

200   She hath despis'd mee rejoycingly, and Ile bee
merry in my Revenge.

ENTER PISANIO

Be those the Garments?

Pisanio   I, my Noble Lord.

Cloten   How long is't since she went to Milford-Haven?

205 **Pisanio**   She can scarse be there yet.

Cloten   Bring this Apparrell to my Chamber, that is
the second thing that I have commanded thee.
                                          The third
is, that thou wilt be a voluntarie Mute to my designe.
                                                      Be
210 but dutious, and true preferment shall tender it selfe to
thee.
      My Revenge is now at Milford, would I had wings
to follow it.
                Come, and be true.

215

[Exit]

Pisanio   Thou bid'st me to my losse: for true to thee,
Were to prove false, which I will never bee
To him that is most true.
                          To Milford go,
And finde not her, whom thou pursuest.
220   Flow, flow
You Heavenly blessings on her: This Fooles speede
Be crost with slownesse; Labour be his meede.

[Exit]

[W][1] F2 and most modern texts = 'insultment', F1 = 'insulment'

Scena Sexta

ENTER IMOGEN ALONE ¹

Imogen   I see a mans life is a tedious one,
I have tyr'd my selfe: and for two nights together
Have made the ground my bed.
                              I should be sicke,
5   But that my resolution helpes me: Milford,
When from the Mountaine top, Pisanio shew'd thee,
Thou was't within a kenne.
                          Oh Jove, I thinke
Foundations flye the wretched: such I meane,
10 Where they should be releev'd.
                          Two Beggers told me,
I could not misse my way.
                          Will poore Folkes lye
That have Afflictions on them, knowing 'tis
15 A punishment, or Triall?
                          Yes; no wonder,
When Rich-ones scarse tell true.
                          To lapse in Fulnesse
Is sorer, then to lye for Neede: and Falshood
20 Is worse in Kings, then Beggers.
                          My deere Lord,
Thou art one o'th'false Ones: Now I thinke on thee,
My hunger's gone; but even before, I was
At point to sinke, for food.
25   But what is this?

Heere is a path too't: 'tis some savage hold:
I were best not call; I dare not call: yet Famine
Ere cleane it o're-throw Nature, makes it valiant.

Plentie, and Peace breeds Cowards: Hardnesse ever
30 Of Hardinesse is Mother.
                          Hoa? who's heere?

If any thing that's civill, speake: if savage,   R 385 - b
Take, or lend.

R 385 - b / L 386 - b : 3.6.1 - 3.6.24

^{SD} ₁ most modern texts add to the stage directions that she is dressed in boy's or young man's clothes, and
appears close to the mouth of the cave-home of Belarius, Guiderius and Arviragus

35   Hoa?
                                No answer?
                                        Then Ile enter.
                    Best draw my Sword; and if mine Enemy
                    But feare the Sword like me, hee'l scarsely looke on't.

                    Such a Foe, good Heavens.

                            [Exit] [1]

SD [1] most modern texts suggest Imogen exits into the cave

Scena Septima

**[Some modern texts do not create a new scene but continue this as part of
Act Three Scene 6]**

ENTER BELARIUS, GUIDERIUS, AND ARVIRAGUS

Belarius	You Polidore have prov'd best Woodman, and
	Are Master of the Feast: Cadwall, and I
	Will play the Cooke, and Servant, 'tis our match:
	The sweat of industry would dry, and dye
5	But for the end it workes too.
	Come, our stomackes
	Will make what's homely, savoury: Wearinesse
	Can snore upon the Flint, when restie Sloth
	Findes the Downe-pillow hard.
10	Now peace be heere,
	Poore house, that keep'st thy selfe. }
Guiderius	I am throughly weary.
Arviragus	I am weake with toyle, yet strong in appetite.
Guiderius	There is cold meat i'th'Cave, we'l brouz on that
15	Whil'st what we have kill'd, be Cook'd.
Belarius	Stay, come not in: ¹
	But that it eates our victualles, I should thinke
	Heere were a Faiery.
Guiderius	What's the matter, Sir? }
20 **Belarius**	By Jupiter an Angell: or if not
	An earthly Paragon.
	Behold Divinenesse
	No elder then a Boy.

ENTER IMOGEN

Imogen	Good masters harme me not:

L 386 - b   :   **3.6.28 - 3.6.45**

¹ most modern texts combine this with the previous short line from Guiderius to form a single split
verse line: however, Ff allow for Belarius to come out from the cave before speaking

25		Before I enter'd heere, I call'd, and thought
		To have begg'd, or bought, what I have took : good troth
		I have stolne nought, nor would not, though I had found
		Gold strew'd i'th'Floore.
		Heere's money for my Meate,
30		I would have left it on the Boord, so soone
		As I had made my Meale ; and parted
		With Pray'rs for the Provider.
	Guiderius	Money?
		Youth.
35	**Arviragus**	All Gold and Silver rather turne to durt,
		As 'tis no better reckon'd, but of those
		Who worship durty Gods.
	Imogen	I see you're angry :
		Know, if you kill me for my fault, I should
40		Have dyed, had I not made it.
	Belarius	Whether bound?
	Imogen	To Milford-Haven.
	Belarius	What's your name?
	Imogen	Fidele Sir : I have a Kinsman, who
45		Is bound for Italy ; he embark'd at Milford,
		To whom being going, almost spent with hunger,
		I am falne in this offence.
	Belarius	Prythee (faire youth)
		Thinke us no Churles : nor measure our good mindes
50		By this rude place we live in.
		Well encounter'd,
		'Tis almost night, you shall have better cheere
		Ere you depart ; and thankes to stay, and eate it :
		Boyes, bid him welcome.
55	**Guiderius**	Were you a woman, youth,
		I should woo hard, but be your Groome in honesty :
		I bid for you, as I do buy. [W1]
	Arviragus	Ile make't my Comfort
		He is a man, Ile love him as my Brother :
60		And such a welcome as I'ld give to him
		(After long absence) such is yours.
		Most welcome :

L 386 - b

L 386 - b / R 386 - b : 3.6.46 - 3.6.73

[W1] Ff = 'I bid for you, as I'ld give to him' : to clarify, modern texts usually set 'Ay' (or I), 'bid for you, as I'ld buy.

82

	Be sprightly, for you fall 'mongst Friends . }
Imogen	'Mongst Friends? [1]
65	If Brothers : would it had bin so, that they
	Had bin my Fathers Sonnes, then had my prize
	Bin lesse, and so more equall ballasting
	To thee Posthumus . }
Belarius	He wrings at some distresse .
70 **Guiderius**	Would I could free't.
Arviragus	Or I, what ere it be, }
	What paine it cost, what danger : Gods !
Belarius	Hearke Boyes . [2] }
Imogen	Great men[3]
75	That had a Court no bigger then this Cave,
	That did attend themselves, and had the vertue
	Which their owne Conscience seal'd them : laying by
	That nothing-guift of differing Multitudes
	Could not out-peere these twaine.
80	Pardon me Gods,
	I'ld change my sexe to be Companion with them,
	Since Leonatus false . }
Belarius	It shall be so :
	Boyes wee'l go dresse our Hunt.
85	Faire youth come in ;
	Discourse is heavy, fasting : when we have supp'd
	Wee'l mannerly demand thee of thy Story,

So farre as thou wilt speake it.

Guiderius	Pray draw neere.
90 **Arviragus**	The Night to'th'Owle, →
	And Morne to th'Larke lesse welcome.
Imogen	Thankes Sir.
Arviragus	I pray draw neere. [4]

[Exeunt]

[A 1] most modern texts indicate this is spoken as an aside

[SD 2] most modern texts add a stage direction here that Belarius draws the two boys aside to whisper

[A 3] most modern texts indicate this is spoken as an aside

[LS 4] this Ff series of short lines presents the most delicate moment in the play, the very strong and puzzled love greetings between two young men and a (supposed) third (all unaware they are brothers and sister): modern regularising by relineation and split-line formation destroys the magical stage fragility

Scena Octava

[Some modern texts refer to this as Act Three Scene 7]

ENTER TWO ROMAN SENATORS, AND TRIBUNES [1]

1st. Senator	This is the tenor of the Emperors Writ;
	That since the common men are now in Action
	'Gainst the Pannonians, and Dalmatians,
	And that the Legions now in Gallia, are
5	Full weake to undertake our Warres against
	The falne-off Britaines, that we do incite
	The Gentry to this businesse.
	He creates
	Lucius Pro-Consull: and to you the Tribunes
10	For this immediate Levy, he commands[2]
	His absolute Commission.
	Long live Cæsar
Tribune	Is Lucius Generall of the Forces?
	}
2nd. Senator	I.
15 **Tribune**	Remaining now in Gallia?
	}
1st. Senator	With those Legions
	Which I have spoke of, whereunto your levie
	Must be suppliant: the words of your Commission
	Will tye you to the numbers, and the time
20	Of their dispatch.
	}
Tribune{s} [3]	We will discharge our duty.

[Exeunt]

R 386 - b : 3.7.1 - 3.7.16

[1] in the Ff nomenclature for this scene, the two Senators are clearly separated by the prefixes 1. Sen and 2. Sen. while the Tribunes are not: thus it is possible that different Tribunes reply at different times in the scene: however, some modern texts give all the Tribunes' responses to a single character they call 1st. Tribune: in this script the Ff lack of titling for the Tribunes will be followed, and readers and actors are invited to imagine the replies as they please

[2] though most modern texts agree with Ff and print this as 'commands', one interesting gloss = 'commends'

[3] the Ff prefix is set as "Tri.' which could be singular or plural, and the line could be spoken by one on behalf of all the Tribunes, or by the several who are there

Actus Quartus. Scena Prima

ENTER CLOTTEN ALONE

Cloten   I am neere to'th'place where they should meet,
if Pisanio have mapp'd it truely.
                              How fit his Garments
serve me?

5   Why should his Mistris who was made by him   R 386 - b
that made the Taylor, not be fit too?
                              The rather (saving
reverence of the Word) for 'tis saide a Womans fitnesse
comes by fits: therein I must play the Workman, I dare

10   speake it to my selfe, for it is not Vainglorie for a man,
and his Glasse, to confer in his owne Chamber; I meane,
the Lines of my body are as well drawne as his; no lesse
young, more strong, not beneath him in Fortunes, beyond him in the advantage of the time, above him in

15   Birth, alike conversant in generall services, and more re-
markeable in single oppositions; yet this imperseverant
Thing loves him in my despight.
                              What Mortalitie is?

Posthumus, thy head (which now is growing uppon thy

20   shoulders) shall within this houre be off, thy Mistris in-
forced, thy Garments cut to peeces before thy[1] face: and
all this done, spurne her home to her Father, who may
(happily) be a little angry for my so rough usage: but my
Mother having power of his testinesse, shall turne all in-

25   to my commendations.
                              My Horse is tyde up safe, out
Sword, and to a sore purpose: Fortune put them in to my
hand: This is the very description of their meeting place
and the Fellow dares not deceive me.

[Exit]

R 386 - b / L 387 - b : 4.1.1 - 4.1.25

[1] Ff and some modern texts = 'thy', other modern texts = 'her'

Scena Secunda

**ENTER BELARIUS, GUIDERIUS, ARVIRAGUS, AND
IMOGEN FROM THE CAVE**

Belarius	[1] You are not well: Remaine heere in the Cave,	
	Wee'l come to you after[2] Hunting.	
		}
Arviragus	Brother, stay heere:	
	Are we not Brothers?	
		}
5 **Imogen**	So man and man should be,	
	But Clay and Clay, differs in dignitie,	
	Whose dust is both alike.	
	I am very sicke,[3]	
Guiderius	Go you to Hunting, Ile abide with him.	
10 **Imogen**	So sicke I am not, yet I am not well:	
	But not so Citizen a wanton, as	
	To seeme to dye, ere sicke: So please you, leave me,	
	Sticke to your Journall course: the breach of Custome,	
	Is breach of all.	
15	I am ill, but your being by me	
	Cannot amend me.	
	Society, is no comfort	
	To one not sociable: I am not very sicke,	
	Since I can reason of it: pray you trust me heere,	
20	Ile rob none but my selfe, and let me dye	
	Stealing so poorely.	
Guiderius	I love thee: I have spoke it,[4]	
	How much the quantity, the waight as much,	
	As I do love my Father.	

WHO [1]
   most modern texts explain the first two speeches are said to Imogen

W [2]
  Ff = 'after', setting a twelve syllable split line: one modern gloss offers 'from' even though this would
  only reduce the line by one syllable

PCT [3]
  Ff = a comma, most modern texts = a period: possibly the comma is intended for Guiderius to
  immediately interrupt Imogen

LS [4]
  most modern texts print this as the second half of a split verse line, presumably implying it comes
  as a quick line from out of the blue, yet there is something equally attractive about two short lines
  which allow for a pause (of awkwardness? embarrassment?) before Guiderius finally manages to speak

25	**Belarius**	What? How? how?
	Arviragus	If it be sinne to say so (Sir) I yoake mee In my good Brothers fault: I know not why
30		I love this youth, and I have heard you say, Love's reasons, without reason. The Beere at doore, And a demand who is't shall dye, I'ld say My Father, not this youth.
	Belarius	Oh noble straine!¹
35		O worthinesse of Nature, breed of Greatnesse!
		"Cowards father Cowards, & Base things Syre Bace; "Nature hath Meale, and Bran; Contempt, and Grace²
		I'me not their Father, yet who this should bee, Doth myracle it selfe, lov'd before mee.
40		'Tis the ninth houre o'th'Morne.
	Arviragus	Brother, farewell.
	Imogen	I wish ye sport.
	Arviragus	You health ⸺ So please you Sir³
	Imogen	These are kinde Creatures. → ⁴
45		Gods, what lyes I have heard: Our Courtiers say, all's savage, but at Court; Experience, oh thou disproov'st Report.
		Th'emperious Seas breeds Monsters; for the Dish, Poore Tributary Rivers, as sweet Fish:
50		I am sicke still, heart-sicke; Pisanio, Ile now taste of thy Drugge. ⁵
	Guiderius	I could not stirre him: ⁶

L 387 - b

L 387 - b / R 387 - b : 4.2.18 - 4.2.38

^A₁ most modern texts indicate this is spoken as an aside

^{PCT}₂ Ff only print the quotation marks at the beginning of the line, most modern texts print them both at the beginning and end of each line

^{SD}₃ most modern texts add stage directions here that Arviragus and Belarius move aside with Guiderius joining them, and thus Imogen's next speech is delivered as an aside

^{SP}₄ arguing white space was responsible for the printing of these 2 short lines, most modern texts reduce them to a single line: however, the moment of realisation for Imogen might well warrant the pause

^{SD}₅ most modern texts add the direction that Imogen takes some of the drug

^{SD}₆ most modern texts indicate this conversation takes place away from Imogen

		He said he was gentle, but unfortunate;
		Dishonestly afflicted, but yet honest.
55	**Arviragus**	Thus did he answer†¹ me: yet said heereafter,
		I might know more.
	Belarius	To'th'Field, to'th'Field:
		Wee'l leave you for this time, go in, and rest.
	Arviragus	Wee'l not be long away.
60	**Belarius**	Pray be not sicke,
		For you must be our Huswife.
	Imogen	Well, or ill,
		I am bound to you.

[Exit] ²

	Belarius	And shal't be ever.
65		This youth, how ere distrest, appeares he³ hath had
		Good Ancestors.
	Arviragus	How Angell-like he sings?
	Guiderius	But his neate Cookerie?
	Arviragus ⁴	He cut our Rootes in Charracters,
70		And sawc'st our Brothes, as Juno had bin sicke,
		And he her Dieter.
	Arviragus	Nobly he yoakes
		A smiling, with a sigh; as if the sighe
		Was that it was, for not being such a Smile:
75		The Smile, mocking the Sigh, that it would flye
		From so divine a Temple, to commix
		With windes, that Saylors raile at.
	Guiderius	I do note,
		That greefe and patience rooted in them⁵ both,
80		Mingle their spurres together.

W₁ F1 = 'auswer', F2 = 'answer'

SD₂ most modern texts add the exit is back into the cave

W₃ Ff = 'appeares he', most modern texts = either 'approves he hath' or 'appears had'

P₄ Ff have assigned both this and the following speech to Arviragus: rather than let him keep both (boyish enthusiasm?) most modern texts give this speech to Guiderius or, more rarely, to Belarius

W₅ Ff = 'them', most modern texts = 'him'

Arviragus	Grow patient,
	And let the stinking-Elder (Greefe) untwine
	His perishing roote, with the encreasing Vine.
Belarius	It is great morning.
85 | Come away: Who's there? [1] |

ENTER CLOTEN

Cloten	I cannot finde those Runnagates, that Villaine
	Hath mock'd me.
	I am faint.
	⟩
Belarius	Those Runnagates?
90	Meanes he not us?
	I partly know him, 'tis
	Cloten, the Sonne o'th'Queene.
	I feare some Ambush:
	I saw him not these many yeares, and yet
95	I know 'tis he: We are held as Out-Lawes: Hence.
Guiderius	He is but one: you, and my Brother search
	What Companies are neere: pray you away,
	Let me alone with him. [2]
	⟩
Cloten	Soft, what are you
100	That flye me thus?
	Some villaine-Mountainers?
	I have heard of such.
	What Slave art thou?
	⟩
Guiderius	A thing
105	More slavish did I ne're, then answering
	A Slave without a knocke.
	⟩
Cloten	Thou art a Robber,
	A Law-breaker, a Villaine: yeeld thee Theefe.
Guiderius	To who? to thee?
110	What art thou?
	Have not I
	An arme as bigge as thine?
	A heart, as bigge:
	Thy words I grant are bigger: for I weare not
115 | My Dagger in my mouth. |

[SD 1] most modern texts add a stage direction here, that the three withdraw to a separate part of the stage

[SD 2] most modern texts add a stage direction here for the exit of Belarius and Arviragus

Say what thou art: R 387 - b
Why I should yeeld to thee?
                                                                }

Cloten   Thou Villaine base,
Know'st me not by my Cloathes?
                                                             }

120 **Guiderius**   No, nor thy Taylor, Rascall:
Who is thy Grandfather?
                                  He made those cloathes,
Which (as it seemes) make thee.
                                                       }

Cloten   Thou precious Varlet,
125   My Taylor made them not.
                                              }

Guiderius   Hence then, and thanke
The man that gave them thee.
                                         Thou art some Foole,
I am loath to beate thee.
                                      }

130 **Cloten**   Thou injurious Theefe,
Heare but my name, and tremble.
                                                 }

Guiderius   What's thy name?

Cloten   Cloten, thou Villaine.

Guiderius   Cloten, thou double Villaine be thy name,
135   I cannot tremble at it, were it Toad, or Adder, Spider,
'Twould move me sooner.
                                      }

Cloten   To thy further feare,
Nay, to thy meere Confusion, thou shalt know
I am Sonne to'th'Queene.

140 **Guiderius**   I am sorry for't: not seeming
So worthy as thy Birth.
                                   }

Cloten   Art not afeard?

Guiderius   Those that I reverence, those I feare: the Wise:
At Fooles I laugh: not feare them.
                                                }

145 **Cloten**   Dye the death:
When I have slaine thee with my proper hand,
Ile follow those that even now fled hence:
And on the Gates of Luds-Towne set your heads:
Yeeld Rusticke Mountaineer.

[Fight and Exeunt]

ENTER BELARIUS AND ARVIRAGUS

150	**Belarius**	No Companie's abroad?
	Arviragus	None in the world: you did mistake him sure.
	Belarius	I cannot tell: Long is it since I saw him,
		But Time hath nothing blurr'd those lines of Favour
		Which then he wore: the snatches in his voice,
155		And burst of speaking were as his: I am absolute
		'Twas very Cloten.
	Arviragus	In this place we left them;
		I wish my Brother make good time with him,
		You say he is so fell.
160	**Belarius**	Being scarse made up,
		I meane to man; he had not apprehension
		Of roaring terrors: For defect of judgement
		Is oft the cause of Feare.

ENTER GUIDERIUS [1]

But see thy Brother.

165	**Guiderius**	This Cloten was a Foole, an empty purse,
		There was no money in't: Not Hercules
		Could have knock'd out his Braines, for he had none:
		Yet I not doing this, the Foole had borne
		My head, as I do his.
170	**Belarius**	What hast thou done?
	Guiderius	I am perfect what: cut off one Clotens head,
		Sonne to the Queene (after his owne report)
		Who call'd me Traitor, Mountaineer, and swore
		With his owne single hand heel'd take us in,
175		Displace our heads, where (thanks the[2] Gods) they grow
		And set them on Luds-Towne.
	Belarius	We are all undone.
	Guiderius	Why, worthy Father, what have we to loose,
		But that he swore to take, our Lives? the Law
180		Protects not us, then why should we be tender,

SD 1 most modern texts note that he is carrying Cloten's head

W 2 F1-2 = 'the', F3 = 'thankes to the', most modern texts = 'ye'

To let an arrogant peece of flesh threat us?
Play Judge, and Executioner, all himselfe?   L 388 - b
For we do feare the Law.
                              What company
185   Discover you abroad?
                              }

Belarius   No single soule
Can we set eye on: but in all safe reason
He must have some Attendants.
                              Though his Honor¹
190   Was nothing but mutation, I, and that
From one bad thing to worse: Not Frenzie,
Not absolute madnesse could so farre have rav'd
To bring him heere alone: although perhaps
It may be heard at Court, that such as wee
195   Cave heere, hunt heere, are Out-lawes, and in time
May make some stronger head, the which he hearing,
(As it is like him) might breake out, and sweare
Heel'd fetch us in, yet is't not probable
To come alone, either he so undertaking,
200   Or they so suffering: then on good ground we feare,
If we do feare this Body hath a taile
More perillous then the head.
                              }

Arviragus   Let Ord'nance
Come as the Gods fore-say it: howsoere,
205   My Brother hath done well.
                              }

Belarius   I had no minde
To hunt this day: The Boy Fideles sickenesse
Did make my way long forth.
                              }

Guiderius   With his owne Sword,
210   Which he did wave against my throat, I have tane

His head from him: Ile throw't into the Creeke
Behinde our Rocke, and let it to the Sea,
And tell the Fishes, hee's the Queenes Sonne, Cloten,
That's all I reake.

[Exit]

215   **Belarius**   I feare 'twill be reveng'd:
Would (Polidore) thou had'st not done't: though valour
Becomes thee well enough.
                              }

ᵂ₁ Ff = 'Honor', most modern texts = 'Humor'

Arviragus	Would I had done't:
	So the Revenge alone pursu'de me: Polidore
220	I love thee brotherly, but envy much
	Thou hast robb'd me of this deed: I would Revenges
	That possible strength might meet, wold seek us through
	And put us to our answer.

Belarius	Well, 'tis done:
225	Wee'l hunt no more to day, nor seeke for danger
	Where there's no profit.
	I prythee to our Rocke,
	You and Fidele play the Cookes: Ile stay
	Till hasty Polidore returne, and bring him
230	To dinner presently.

Arviragus	Poore sicke Fidele.
	Ile willingly to him, to gaine his colour,
	Il'd let a parish of such Clotens blood,
	And praise my selfe for charity.

[Exit]

235	**Belarius**	Oh thou Goddesse,
		Thou divine Nature; thou' thy selfe thou blazon'st
		In these two Princely Boyes: they are as gentle
		As Zephires blowing below the Violet,
		Not wagging his sweet head; and yet, as rough
240		(Their Royall blood enchaf'd) as the rud'st winde,
		That by the top doth take the Mountaine Pine,
		And make him stoope to th'Vale.
		'Tis wonder
		That an invisible instinct should frame them
245		To Royalty unlearn'd, Honor untaught,
		Civility not seene from other: valour
		That wildely growes in them, but yeelds a crop
		As if it had beene sow'd: yet still it's strange
		What Clotens being heere to us portends,
250		Or what his death will bring us.

ENTER GUIDEREUS

Guiderius	Where's my Brother?	R 388 - b
	I have sent Clotens Clot-pole downe the streame,	
	In Embassie to his Mother; his Bodie's hostage	
	For his returne.	

[Solemn Musick]

^W1 Ff = 'thou', most modern texts = 'how'

255	**Belarius**	My ingenuous Instrument,
		(Hearke Polidore) it sounds: but what occasion
		Hath Cadwal now to give it motion?
		Hearke.

	Guiderius	Is he at home?
		}
260	**Belarius**	He went hence even now.

	Guiderius	What does he meane?→[1]
		Since death of my deer'st Mother
		It did not speake before.
		All solemne things
265		Should answer solemne Accidents.
		The matter?
		Triumphes for nothing, and lamenting Toyes,
		Is jollity for Apes, and greefe for boyes.
		Is Cadwall mad?

**ENTER ARVIRAGUS, WITH IMOGEN DEAD, BEARING
HER IN HIS ARMES**

270	**Belarius**	Looke, heere he comes,
		And brings the dire occasion in his Armes,
		Of what we blame him for.
		}

	Arviragus	The Bird is dead
		That we have made so much on.
275		I had rather
		Have skipt from sixteene yeares of Age, to sixty:
		To have turn'd my leaping time into a Crutch,
		Then have seene this.
		}

	Guiderius	Oh sweetest, fayrest Lilly:
280		My Brother weares thee not the[2] one halfe so well,
		As when thou grew'st thy selfe.
		}

	Belarius	Oh Melancholly,
		Who ever yet could sound thy bottome?
		Finde
285		The Ooze, to shew what Coast thy sluggish care[3]
		Might'st easilest harbour in.

L 389 - b : 4.2.186 - 4.2.206

[SP1] most modern texts print these two short Ff lines as one complete line: however, the enormity of
hearing the music and the solemn memories it evokes could well justify the pause from Ff as set

[W2] Ff = 'the', some modern texts omit the word, possibly to maintain the line as purely metric

[W3] Ff = 'care', some modern texts = 'crare' (a term for a small boat, thus keeping to the sailing image)

                      Thou blessed thing,
Jove knowes what man thou might'st[1] have made: but I,
Thou dyed'st a most rare Boy, of Melancholly.

290 How found you him?
                         }

Arviragus Starke, as you see:
Thus smiling, as some Fly had tickled slumber,
Not as deaths dart being laugh'd at: his right Cheeke
Reposing on a Cushion.
                       }

295 **Guiderius** Where?
                      }

Arviragus O'th'floore:
His armes thus leagu'd, I thought he slept, and put
My clowted Brogues from off my feete, whose rudenesse
Answer'd my steps too lowd.
                    }

300 **Guiderius** Why, he but sleepes:
If he be gone, hee'l make his Grave, a Bed:
With female Fayries will his Tombe be haunted,
And Wormes will not come to thee.
                    }

Arviragus With fayrest Flowers
305 Whil'st Sommer lasts, and I live heere, Fidele,
Ile sweeten thy sad grave: thou shalt not lacke
The Flower that's like thy face.[2]
                     Pale-Primrose, nor
The azur'd Hare-bell, like thy Veines: no, nor
310 The leafe of Eglantine, whom not to slander,
Out-sweetned not thy breath: the Raddocke[3] would
With Charitable bill (Oh bill sore shaming
Those rich-left-heyres, that let their Fathers lye
Without a Monument) bring thee all this,
315 Yea, and furr'd Mosse besides.
                    When Flowres are none
To winter-ground[4] thy Coarse ——
                    }

Guiderius Prythee have done,
And do not play in Wench-like words with that
320 Which is so serious.

L 389 - b : 4.2.207- 4.2.231

[PCT] [1] Ff = 'might'st', some modern texts = 'might'

[W] [2] Ff set a period, as if the emotion is getting the better of Arviragus, and he needs the break to regain
self-control: most modern texts reduce the moment by setting a comma

[W] [3] Ff = 'Raddocke', some modern texts = 'Ruddocke' (a name for the English bird, the robin redbreast)

[W] [4] Ff and some modern texts = 'winter-ground', others = either 'winter-gown' or 'winter-grown'

		Let us bury him,	
		And not protract with admiration, what	
		Is now due debt.	
		To'th'grave.	
		}	
325	**Arviragus**	Say, where shall's lay him?	L 389 - b
	Guiderius	By good Euriphile, our Mother.	
		}	
	Arviragus	Bee't so:	

	Arviragus	Bee't so:
		And let us (Polidore) though now our voyces
		Have got the mannish cracke, sing him to'th'ground
330		As once to[1] our Mother: use like note, and words,
		Save that Euriphile, must be Fidele.
		}

	Guiderius	Cadwall,
		I cannot sing: Ile weepe, and word it with thee;
		For Notes of sorrow, out of tune, are worse
335		Then Priests, and Phanes that lye.
		}

	Arviragus	Wee'l speake it then.

	Belarius	Great greefes I see med'cine the lesse: For Cloten
		Is quite forgot.
		He was a Queenes Sonne, Boyes,
340		And though he came our enemy remember
		He was paid for that: though meane, and mighty rotting
		Together have one dust, yet Reverence
		(That Angell of the world) doth make distinction
		Of place 'tweene high, and low.
345		Our Foe was Princely,
		And though you tooke his life, as being our Foe,
		Yet bury him, as a Prince.
		}

	Guiderius	Pray you fetch him hither,
		Thersites body is as good as Ajax,
350		When neyther are alive.
		}

	Arviragus	If you'l go fetch him,
		Wee'l say our Song the whil'st: [2] Brother begin.

	Guiderius	Nay Cadwall, we must lay his head to th'East,
		My Father hath a reason for't.
		}

355	**Arviragus**	'Tis true.

L 389 - b / R 389 - b : 4.2.232 - 4.2.256

[W][1] Ff = 'to' a few modern texts remove the word to preserve the pentameter

[SD][2] most modern texts add a stage direction here to give an exit for Belarius

Guiderius		Come on then, and remove him.
Arviragus		So, begin. }

SONG [1]

	Guiderius	***Feare no more the heate o'th'Sun,***
		Nor the furious Winters rages,
360		***Thou thy worldly task hast don,***
		Home art gon, and tane thy wages.
		Golden Lads, and Girles all must,
		As Chimney-Sweepers comes to dust.
	Arviragus	***Feare no more the frowne o'th'Great,***
365		***Thou art past the Tirants stroake,***
		Care no more to cloath and eate,
		To thee the Reede is as the Oake:
		The Scepter, Learning, Physicke must,
		All follow this and come to dust.
370	**Guiderius**	***Feare no more the Lightning flash.***
	Arviragus	***Nor th'all-dreaded Thunderstone.***
	Guiderius	***Feare not Slander, Censure rash.***
	Arviragus	***Thou hast finish'd Joy and mone.***
	Both	*All Lovers young, all Lovers must,*
375		*Consigne to thee and come to dust.*
	Guiderius	*No Exorcisor harme thee,*
	Arviragus	***Nor no witch-craft charme thee.***
	Guiderius	***Ghost unlaid forbeare thee.***
	Arviragus	***Nothing ill come neere thee.***
380	**Both**	***Quiet consumation have,***
		And renowned be thy grave.

ENTER BELARIUS WITH THE BODY OF CLOTEN

Guiderius		We have done our obsequies: [2]→
		Come lay him downe.
Belarius		Heere's a few Flowres, but 'bout midnight more:
385		The hearbes that have on them cold dew o'th'night
		Are strewings fit'st for Graves: upon their Faces [3]

R 389 - b : 4.2.257 - 4.2.285

LS [1] the individual lines are as found in Ff, the grouping into four 6 line verses follows modern practice

SP [2] most modern texts print these two short Ff lines as one complete line: however, the emotion of the moment well warrants the pause as indicated by the original text

W [3] though most modern texts agree with Ff and print this as 'their Faces', one gloss = 'th'earths face'

You were as Flowres, now wither'd: even so
These Herbelets shall, which we upon you strew.

Come on, away, apart upon our knees:
390   The ground that gave them first, ha's them againe:
Their pleasures here are past, so are[1] their paine.

[Exeunt] [2]

R 389 - b

IMOGEN AWAKES

Yes Sir, to Milford-Haven, which is the way?

I thanke you: by yond bush? pray how farre thether?

'Ods pittikins: can it be sixe mile yet?

395   I have gone all night: 'Faith, Ile lye downe, and sleepe.

But soft; no Bedfellow?[3]
               Oh Gods, and Goddesses!

These Flowres are like the pleasures of the World;
This bloody man the care on't.
400   I hope I dreame:
For so I thought I was a Cave-keeper,
And Cooke to honest Creatures.
                  But 'tis not so:
'Twas but a bolt of nothing, shot at nothing,
405   Which the Braine makes of Fumes.
                     Our very eyes,
Are sometimes like our Judgements,[†4] blinde.
                       Good faith

I tremble still with feare: but if there be
410   Yet left in Heaven, as small a drop of pittie
As a Wrens eye; fear'd Gods, a part of it.
The Dreame's heere still: even when I wake it is
Without me, as within me: not imagin'd, felt.

A headlesse man?
                  The Garments of Posthumus?
415

I know the shape of's Legge: this is his Hand:
His Foote Mercuriall: his martiall Thigh
The brawnes of Hercules : but his Joviall face——

R 389 - b / L 390 - b : 4.2.286 - 4.2.311

[W1] Ff = 'are', most modern texts = 'is'
[SD2] most modern texts add to the stage direction that Imogen remains, and it is she who starts to speak
[SD3] most modern texts rightly suggest this is when she sees the body, but readers/actors should note
she doesn't say anything about it being headless or dressed in Posthumus' clothes for another twelve lines
[PCT4] F1 sets a blur which could be a comma or a colon: F2/most modern texts set a comma

Murther in heaven?
420   How? 'tis gone.
                      Pisanio,
All Curses madded Hecuba gave the Greekes,
And mine to boot, be darted on thee: thou
Conspir'd with that Irregulous divell Cloten,
425 Hath heere cut off my Lord.
                   To write, and read,
Be henceforth treacherous.
                 Damn'd Pisanio,
Hath with his forged Letters (damn'd Pisanio)
430 From this most bravest vessell of the world
Strooke the maine top!
              Oh Posthumus, alas,
Where is thy head? where's that?
Aye me! where's that?
435 Pisanio might have kill'd thee at the heart,
And left this[1] head on.
              How should this be, Pisanio?
'Tis he, and Cloten: Malice, and Lucre in them
Have laid this Woe heere.
440   Oh 'tis pregnant, pregnant!
The Drugge he gave me, which hee said was precious
And Cordiall to me, have I not found it
Murd'rous to'th'Senses?
            That confirmes it home:
445 This is Pisanio's deede, and Cloten: Oh!
Give colour to my pale cheeke with thy blood,
That we the horrider may seeme to those
Which chance to finde us. [2]
         Oh, my Lord! my Lord! [3]

ENTER LUCIUS, CAPTAINES, AND A SOOTHSAYER

450 **Captaine**   To them, the Legions garrison'd in Gallia
After your will, have crost the Sea, attending
You heere at Milford-Haven, with your Shippes:
They are heere[4] in readinesse.

Lucius   But what from Rome?

---

[1] Ff and some modern texts = 'this', other modern texts = 'thy'

[2] most modern texts add the stage direction that here Imogen smears her cheeks with blood

[3] most modern texts suggest Imogen faints and/or falls on the body

[4] F1 and some modern texts = 'heere', F2 omits the word, other modern texts = 'hence'

99

455	**Captaine**	The Senate hath stirr'd up the Confiners,
		And Gentlemen of Italy, most willing Spirits,
		That promise Noble Service: and they come
		Under the Conduct of bold Iachimo,
		Syenna's Brother.
460	**Lucius**	When expect you them?
	Captaine	With the next benfit o'th'winde.
	Lucius	This forwardnesse
		Makes our hopes faire.
		Command our present numbers
465		Be muster'd: bid the Captaines looke too't.
		Now Sir,
		What have you dream'd of late of this warres purpose.
	Soothsayer	Last night the very Gods shew'd me a vision
		(I fast, and pray'd for their Intelligence) thus:
470		I saw Joves Bird, the Roman Eagle wing'd
		From the spungy South, to this part of the West,
		There vanish'd in the Sun-beames, which portends
		(Unlesse my sinnes abuse my Divination)
		Successe to th'Roman hoast.
475	**Lucius**	Dreame often so,
		And never false.
		Soft hoa, what truncke is heere?
		Without his top?
		The ruine speakes, that sometime
480		It was a worthy[†1] building.
		How? a Page?
		Or dead, or sleeping on him?
		But dead rather:
		For Nature doth abhorre to make his bed
485		With the defunct, or sleepe upon the dead.
		Let's see the Boyes face.
	Captaine	Hee's alive my Lord.
	Lucius	Hee'l then instruct us of this body: Young one,
		Informe us of thy Fortunes, for it seemes
490		They crave to be demanded: who is this
		Thou mak'st thy bloody Pillow?
		Or who was he

L 390 - b

L 390 - b / R 390 - b : 4.2.337 - 4.2.363

[W1] [†1]F1 = 'wort hy', F2 = 'worthy'

		That (otherwise then noble Nature did)
		Hath alter'd that good Picture?
495		What's thy interest
		In this sad wracke?
		How came't?
		Who is't?
		What art thou?

500	**Imogen**	I am nothing; or if not,
		Nothing to be were better: This was my Master,
		A very valiant Britaine, and a good,
		That heere by Mountaineers lyes slaine: Alas,
		There is no more such Masters: I may wander
505		From East to Occident, cry out for Service,
		Try many, all good: serve truly: never
		Finde such another Master.

	Lucius	'Lacke, good youth:
		Thou mov'st no lesse with thy complaining, then
510		Thy Maister in bleeding: say his name, good Friend.

	Imogen	Richard du Champ: [1] If I do lye, and do
		No harme by it, though the Gods heare, I hope
		They'l pardon it.
		Say you Sir?

515	**Lucius**	Thy name?

	Imogen	Fidele Sir.

	Lucius	Thou doo'st approve thy selfe the very same:
		Thy Name well fits thy Faith; thy Faith, thy Name:
		Wilt take thy chance with me?
520		I will not say
		Thou shalt be so well master'd, but be sure
		No lesse belov'd.
		The Romane Emperors Letters
		Sent by a Consull to me, should not sooner
525		Then thine owne worth preferre thee: Go with me.

	Imogen	Ile follow Sir.
		But first, and't please the Gods,
		Ile hide my Master from the Flies, as deepe
		As these poore Pickaxes can digge: and when
530		With wild wood-leaves & weeds, I ha'strew'd his grave

---

[1] most modern texts indicate the remainder of this sentence is spoken as an aside

And on it said a Century of prayers
(Such as I can) twice o're, Ile weepe, and sighe,
And leaving so his service, follow you,
So please you entertaine mee.
                                              }

535   **Lucius**   I good youth,
And rather Father thee, then Master thee: My Friends,
The Boy hath taught us manly duties: Let us
Finde out the prettiest Dazied-Plot we can,
And make him with our Pikes and Partizans
540   A Grave: Come, Arme him: Boy hee's[1] preferr'd
By thee, to us, and he shall be interr'd
As Souldiers can.
                                    Be cheerefull; wipe thine eyes,
Some Falles are meanes the happier to arise.

[Exeunt] [2]

[W1] Ff = 'hee's', some modern texts = 'he is' to extend the line to a pentameter
[SD2] most modern texts add a note that they take Cloten's body off with them

Scena Tertia

ENTER CYMBELINE, LORDS, AND PISANIO

Cymbeline
Againe: and bring[†1] me word how 'tis with her,[2]
A Feavour with the absence of her Sonne; R 390-b
A madnesse, of which her life's in danger: Heavens,
How deeply you at one do touch me.
Imogen,
The great part of my comfort, gone: My Queene
Upon a desperate bed, and in a time
When fearefull Warres point at me: Her Sonne gone,
So needfull for this present?
It strikes me, past
The hope of comfort.
But for thee, Fellow,
Who needs must know of her departure, and
Dost seeme so ignorant, wee'l enforce it from thee
By a sharpe Torture.

Pisanio
Sir, my life is yours,
I humbly set it at your will: But for my Mistris,
I nothing know where she remaines: why gone,
Nor when she purposes returne.
Beseech your Highnes,
Hold me your loyall Servant.

Lord[3]
Good my Liege,
The day that she was missing, he was heere;
I dare be bound hee's true, and shall performe
All parts of his subjection loyally.
For Cloten,
There wants no diligence in seeking him,
And will no doubt be found.

Cymbeline
The time is troublesome:[4]

R 390 - b / L 391 - b : 4.3.1 - 4.3.21

W 1 F1 = 'hring', F2 = 'bring'

SD 2 most modern texts add a stage direction here of an exit for at least one Lord

P 3 as with the Tribunes in Act Three Scene 8, no speech prefixes are given to delineate the Lords, thus these speeches could be assigned to one character (as most modern texts do, i.e. 1st. Lord) or be split between them all

WHO 4 some modern texts explain that the remainder of this speech is delivered to Pisanio

30		Wee'l slip you for a season, but our jealousie Do's yet depend.
	Lord	So please your Majesty, [1] } The Romaine Legions, all from Gallia drawne, Are landed on your Coast, with a supply
35		Of Romaine Gentlemen, by the Senate sent.
	Cymbeline	Now for the Counsaile of my Son and Queen, I am amaz'd with matter. }
	Lord	Good my Liege, Your preparation can affront no lesse
40		Then what you heare of.

                                     Come more, for more you're ready: [†]

    The want is, but to put those Powres in motion,
That long to move.

	Cymbeline	I thanke you: let's withdraw }
45		And meete the Time, as it seekes us.

                                        We feare not

What can from Italy annoy us, but
We greeve at chances heere.

                            Away.

[Exeunt] [2]

50	**Pisanio**	I heard no Letter from my Master, since I wrote him Imogen was slaine.

                                   'Tis strange:

Nor heare I from my Mistris, who did promise
To yeeld me often tydings.

                                Neither know I

55   What is betide to Cloten, but remaine
Perplext in all.

                      The Heavens still must worke:

Wherein I am false, I am honest: not true, to be true.

60   These present warres shall finde I love my Country,
Even to the note o'th'King, or Ile fall in them:
All other doubts, by time let them be cleer'd,
Fortune brings in some Boats, that are not steer'd.

[Exit]

SD [1]
    some modern texts give this Lord a separate entry here, as if the news has just been delivered:
however, Ff's reading suggests the Lord has been on stage since the group entry and that therefore this is
a pressing problem which was understood at the top of the scene and needs swift resolution - something
that initially Cymbeline seems incapable of

SD [2]
    some modern texts add to the stage direction here that all but Pisanio exit

Scena Quarta

ENTER BELARIUS, GUIDERIUS, & ARVIRAGUS

Guiderius	The noyse is round about us.
Belarius	Let us from it.
Arviragus	What pleasure Sir, we finde [1] in life, to locke it From Action, and Adventure.
5 **Guiderius**	Nay, what hope Have we in hiding us? This way the Romaines Must, or for Britaines slay us or receive us For barbarous and unnaturall Revolts 10 During their use, and slay us after.
Belarius	Sonnes, L 391 - b Wee'l higher to the Mountaines, there secure us[†2] To the Kings party there's no going: newnesse Of Clotens death (we being not knowne, not muster'd 15 Among the Bands) may drive us to a render Where we have liv'd; and so extort from's that Which we have done, whose answer would be death Drawne on with Torture.
Guiderius	This is (Sir) a doubt 20 In such a time, nothing becomming you, Nor satisfying us.
Arviragus	It is not likely, That when they heare their[3] Roman horses neigh, Behold their quarter'd Fires; [4] have both their eyes 25 And [†5] eares so cloyd importantly as now,

---

[W1]   F2 and most modern texts = 'finde we', F1 = 'we finde'

[W2]   F2 and most modern texts = 'us' with punctuation following, F1 = 'u..'

[W3]   Ff = 'their', some modern texts = 'the'

[W4]   Ff = 'Fires', some modern texts = 'Files'

[W5]   F2 and most modern texts = 'And', F1 = 'Aud'

		That they will waste their time upon our note,
		To know from whence we are.
		}
	Belarius	Oh, I am knowne
		Of many in the Army: Many yeeres
30		(Though Cloten then but young) you see, not wore him
		From my remembrance.
		And besides, the King
		Hath not deserv'd my Service, nor your Loves,
		Who finde in my Exile, the want of Breeding;
35		The certainty of this heard [1] life, aye hopelesse
		To have the courtesie your Cradle promis'd,
		But to be still hot Summers Tanlings, and
		The shrinking Slaves of Winter.
		}
	Guiderius	Then be so,
40		Better to cease to be.
		Pray Sir, to'th'Army:
		I, and my Brother are not knowne; your selfe
		So out of thought, and thereto so ore-growne,
		Cannot be question'd.
		}
45	**Arviragus**	By this Sunne that shines
		Ile thither: What thing is't, [2] that I never
		Did see man dye, scarse everlook'd on blood,
		But that of Coward Hares, hot Goats, and Venison?
		Never bestrid a Horse, save one, that had
50		A Rider like my selfe, who ne're wore Rowell,
		Nor Iron on his heele?
		I am asham'd
		To looke upon the holy Sunne, to have
		The benefit of his blest Beames, remaining
55		So long a poore unknowne.
		}
	Guiderius	By heavens Ile go,
		If you will blesse me Sir, and give me leave,
		Ile take the better care: but if you will not,
		The hazard therefore due fall on me, by
60		The hands of Romaines.
		}
	Arviragus	So say I, Amen.
	Belarius	No reason I (since of your lives you set
		So slight a valewation) should reserve
		My crack'd one to more care.

[w1] F1 = 'heard', F2 and most modern texts = 'hard'

[w2] F1 = 'is't', F2 = 'is it'

65   Have with you Boyes:
If in your Country warres you chance to dye,
That is my Bed too (Lads) and there Ile lye.

Lead, lead; [1] the time seems long, their blood thinks scorn
Till it flye out and shew them Princes borne.

[Exeunt]

R 391 - b : 4.4.50 - 4.4.54

[A] [1] most modern texts indicate the remainder of this speech is spoken as an aside

Actus Quintus. Scena Prima

ENTER POSTHUMUS ALONE ¹

Posthumus   Yea bloody cloth, Ile keep thee: for I am wisht ²
Thou should'st be colour'd thus.
                                        You married ones,
If each of you should take this course, how many
5   Must murther Wives much better then themselves   R 391 - b
For wrying but a little?
                              Oh Pisanio,
Every good Servant do's not all Commands:
No Bond, but to do just ones.
10   Gods, if you
Should have 'tane vengeance on my faults, I never
Had liv'd to put on this: so had you saved
The noble Imogen, to repent, and strooke
Me (wretch) more worth your Vengeance.
15   But alacke,
You snatch some hence for little faults; that's love
To have them fall no more: you some permit
To second illes with illes, each elder worse,
And make them dread it, to the dooers thrift.

20   But Imogen is your owne, do your best ³ willes,
And make me blest to obey.
                              I am brought hither
Among th'Italian Gentry, and to fight
Against my Ladies Kingdome: 'Tis enough
25   That (Britaine) I have kill'd thy Mistris: Peace, ⁴
Ile give no wound to thee: therefore good Heavens,
Heare patiently my purpose.

R 391 - b / L 392 - b   :   5.1.1 - 5.1.22

^{SD} 1 most modern texts add further information to this stage direction indicating that he is in some
identifiable form of Italian (as opposed to English) clothing, and that he is carrying a bloodied piece of
clothing, from the supposedly dead Imogen, sent him by Pisanio, as ordered

^W 2 though most modern texts agree with Ff and print this as 'am wisht', one gloss = 'once wished'

^W 3 though most modern texts agree with Ff and print this as 'best', one gloss = 'blest'

^W 4 though most modern texts agree with Ff and print this as 'Mistris: Peace', one gloss = 'Mistris-Peace'

                              Ile disrobe me
Of these Italian weedes, and suite my selfe

30   As do's a Britaine Pezant: [1] so Ile fight
Against the part I come with: so Ile dye
For thee (O Imogen) even for whom my life
Is every breath, a death: and thus, unknowne,
Pittied, not hated, to the face of perill

35   My selfe Ile dedicate.
                        Let me make men know
More valour in me, then my habits show.

Gods, put the strength o'th' Leonati in me:
To shame the guize o'th'world, I will begin,[2]

40   The fashion lesse without, and more within.

                  [Exit]

L 392 - b : 5.1.22 - 5.1.33

SD [1] one modern text, rather peculiarly, directs him to change clothes at this point in the speech

PCT [2] most modern texts move the comma from here to after 'The fashion' in the next line

Scena Secunda

**ENTER LUCIUS, IACHIMO, AND THE ROMANE ARMY AT ONE DOORE:
AND THE BRITAINE ARMY AT ANOTHER: LEONATUS POSTHUMUS
FOLLOWING LIKE A POORE SOULDIER. THEY MARCH OVER, AND GOE
OUT. THEN ENTER AGAINE IN SKIRMISH IACHIMO AND POSTHU-
MUS: HE VANQUISHETH AND DISARMETH IACHIMO, AND THEN
LEAVES HIM**

Iachimo	The heavinesse and guilt within my bosome,
	Takes off my manhood: I have belyed a Lady,
	The Princesse of this Country; and the ayre on't
	Revengingly enfeebles me, or could this Carle,
5	A very drudge of Natures, have subdu'de me
	In my profession?
	Knighthoods, and Honors borne
	(As I weare mine) †1 are titles but of scorne.
	If that thy Gentry (Britaine) go before
10	This Lowt, as he exceeds our Lords, the oddes
	Is, that we scarse are men, and you are Goddes.

**[Exit]
THE BATTAILE CONTINUES, THE BRITAINES FLY, CYMBELINE IS
TAKEN: THEN ENTER TO HIS RESCUE, BELLARIUS, GUIDERIUS,
AND ARVIRAGUS**

Belarius	Stand, stand, we have th'advantage of the ground,
	The Lane is guarded: Nothing rowts us, but
	The villany of our feares.
	}
15 **Guiderius** [&] **Arviragus**	Stand, stand, and fight.

**ENTER POSTHUMUS, AND SECONDS THE BRITAINES. THEY RESCUE
CYMBELINE, AND EXEUNT.
THEN ENTER LUCIUS, IACHIMO, AND IMOGEN**

Lucius	Away boy from the Troopes, and save thy selfe:	
	For friends kil friends, and the disorder's such	L 392 - b
	As warre were hood-wink'd.	
	}	

PCT 1
  F1 shows no start to this bracket: F2 and most modern texts show it at the start of the phrase

Iachimo   'Tis their fresh supplies.

20   **Lucius**   It is a day turn'd strangely: or betimes
Let's re-inforce, or fly.

[Exeunt]

Scena Tertia

ENTER POSTHUMUS,[1] AND A BRITAINE LORD

Lord	Cam'st thou from where they made the stand?
Posthumus	I did,
	Though you it seemes come from the Fliers?
Lord	[2] I did.

5   **Posthumus**   No blame be to you sir, for all was lost,
But that the Heavens fought: the King himselfe
Of his wings destitute, the Army broken,
And but the backes of Britaines seene; all flying
Through a strait Lane, the Enemy full-hearted,
10   Lolling the Tongue with slaught'ring: having worke
More plentifull, then Tooles to doo't: strooke downe
Some mortally, some slightly touch'd, some falling
Meerely through feare, that the strait passe was damm'd
With deadmen, hurt behinde, and Cowards living
15   To dye with length'ned shame.

Lord   Where was this Lane?

Posthumus   Close by the battell, ditch'd, & wall'd with turph,
Which gave advantage to an ancient Soldiour
(An honest one I warrant) who deserv'd
20   So long a breeding, as his white beard came to,
In doing this for's Country.
                              Athwart the Lane,
He, with two striplings (Lads more like to run
The Country base, then to commit such slaughter,
25   With faces fit for Maskes, or rather fayrer
Then those for preservation cas'd, or shame)
Made good the passage, cryed to those that fled.

R 392 - b   :   5.3.1 - 5.3.23

[SD 1] most modern texts add that he is now in recognisable English clothing

[LS 2] though Ff set this short speech, some modern texts omit it - claiming it repeats Posthumus' phrase
from a line and a half earlier

Our Britaines hearts[1] dye flying, not our[2] men,
To darknesse fleete soules that flye backwards; stand,
30 Or we are Romanes, and will give you that
Like beasts, which you shun beastly, and may save
But to looke backe in frowne: Stand, stand.

These three,

Three thousand confident, in acte as many:
35 For three performers are the File, when all
The rest do nothing.

With this word stand, stand,

Accomodated by the Place; more Charming
With their owne Noblenesse, which could have turn'd
40 A Distaffe, to a Lance, guilded pale lookes;
Part shame, part spirit renew'd, that some turn'd coward
But by example (Oh a sinne in Warre,
Damn'd in the first beginners) gan to looke
The way that they did, and to grin like Lyons
45 Upon the Pikes o'th'Hunters.

Then beganne

A stop i'th'Chaser; a Retyre: Anon
A Rowt, confusion thicke: forthwith they flye
Chickens, the way which they stopt[3] Eagles: Slaves
50 The strides the[4] Victors made: and now our Cowards
Like Fragments in hard Voyages became
The life o'th'need: having found the backe doore open
Of the unguarded hearts: heavens, how they wound,
Some slaine before some dying; some their Friends
55 Ore-borne i'th'former wave, ten chac'd by one,
Are now each one the slaughter-man of twenty:
Those that would dye, or ere resist, are growne
The mortall bugs o'th'Field.

⟩   R 392 - b

Lord   This was strange chance:
60   A narrow Lane, an old man, and two Boyes.

Posthumus   Nay, do not[5] wonder at it: [6] you are made
                  Rather to wonder at the things you heare,
                  Then to worke any.

[w1] Ff = 'hearts', most modern texts = 'harts', thus calling the fleeing men cowards

[w2] Ff = 'our', one modern gloss suggests 'her'

[w3] Ff = 'stopt', some modern texts = 'stoop't'

[w4] Ff = 'the', some modern texts = 'they'

[w5] Ff = 'not', some modern texts = 'but' (at least one text keeps the 'not' and adds 'yet' to the next phrase)

[w6] for clarity, commentators suggest adding 'yet' or 'though'

Will you Rime upon't,

65 And vent it for a Mock'rie?

Heere is one:

"Two Boyes, an Oldman (twice a Boy) a Lane ,
"Preserv'd the Britaines, was the Romanes bane . [1]

Lord   Nay, be not angry Sir .

}

70 **Posthumus**   Lacke, to what end?

Who dares not stand his Foe, Ile be his Friend :
For if hee'l do, as he is made to doo,
I know hee'l quickly flye my friendship too.

You have put me into Rime .

}

75 **Lord**   Farewell, you're angry.

[Exit]

Posthumus   Still going?

This is a Lord : Oh Noble misery
To be i'th'Field, and aske what newes of me :
To day, how many would have given their Honours
80 To have sav'd their Carkasses? Tooke heele to doo't,
And yet dyed too .

I, in mine owne woe charm'd
Could not finde death, where I did heare him groane,
Nor feele him where he strooke .

85 Being an ugly Monster,
'Tis strange he hides him in fresh Cups, soft Beds,
Sweet words ; or hath moe ministers then we
That draw his knives i'th'War .

Well I will finde him :
90 For being now a Favourer to the Britaine,
No more a Britaine, I have resum'd againe
The part I came in .

Fight I will no more,
But yeeld me to the veriest Hinde, that shall
95 Once touch my shoulder .

Great the slaughter is
Heere made by'th'Romane ; great the Answer be
Britaines must take .

For me, my Ransome's death,
100 On eyther side I come to spend my breath ;
Which neyther heere Ile keepe, nor beare agen,
But end it by some meanes for Imogen .

L 393 - b : 5.3.55 - 5.3.83

[PCT] [1] Ff add quotation marks to the beginning of these two rhyming lines (as if Posthumus were
improvising a rhyme), but not the end : most modern texts add quotation marks at the end of each line too

ENTER TWO CAPTAINES, AND SOLDIERS

1st. Captaine	Great Jupiter be prais'd, Lucius is taken,
	'Tis thought the old man, and his sonnes, were Angels.
105 **2nd. Captaine**	There was a fourth man, in a silly habit,
	That gave th'Affront with them.

}

1st. Captaine	So 'tis reported:
	But none of 'em can be found.

                                 Stand, who's there?

110 **Posthumus**	A Roman,
	Who had not now beene drooping heere, if Seconds
	Had answer'd him.

}

2nd. Captaine	Lay hands on him: a Dogge,
	A legge of Rome shall not returne to tell
115	What Crows have peckt them here: he brags his service
	As if he were of note: bring him to'th'King.

ENTER CYMBELINE, BELARIUS, GUIDERIUS, ARVIRAGUS, PISANIO, AND ROMANE CAPTIVES. THE CAPTAINES PRESENT POSTHUMUS TO CYMBELINE, WHO DELIVERS HIM OVER TO A GAOLER [1]

L 393 - b : 5.3.84 - 5.3.94

SD/P [1] because of the requirements in the next scene, some modern texts add a Second Gaoler and have both Gaolers lock Posthumus in leg-irons (for the possible Ff handling of this, see footnote #1 on the next page): the same modern texts usually continue the next Ff scene as part of Act Five Scene 2

Scena Quarta

**{Some modern texts treat this scene as an extension of Act Five Scene 3
arguing the stage action is continuous]**

ENTER POSTHUMUS, AND GAOLER [1]

Gaoler	You shall not now be stolne, →[2]
	You have lockes upon you:
	So graze, as you finde Pasture.
	}
2nd. Gaoler	I, or a stomacke. [3]

5 **Posthumus** Most welcome bondage; for thou art a way
(I thinke) to liberty: yet am I better
Then one that's sicke o'th'Gowt, since he had rather   L 393 - b
Groane so in perpetuity, then be cur'd
By'th'sure Physitian, Death; who is the key
10 T'unbarre these Lockes.
                    My Conscience, thou art fetter'd
More then my shanks, & wrists: you good Gods give me
The penitent Instrument to picke that Bolt,
Then free for ever.
15   Is't enough I am sorry?
So Children temporall Fathers do appease;
Gods are more full of mercy.
                    Must I repent,
I cannot do it better then in Gyves,
20 Desir'd, more then constrain'd, to satisfie
If of my Freedome 'tis the maine part, take
No stricter render of me, then my All.

I know you are more clement then vilde men,
Who of their broken Debtors take a third,
25 A sixt, a tenth, letting them thrive againe
On their abatement; that's not my desire.

L 393 - b / R 393 - b : 5.4.1 - 5.4.21

SD 1 though two different Gaolers speak in the scene, Ff only show one as entering with Posthumus

LS 2 arguing white space was responsible, most modern texts print these two short Ff lines as one
complete line: however, the Ff layout may give the necessary pauses for the Gaolers to put the
leg-irons on Posthumus

SD 3 most modern texts add a stage direction here for the exit of both Gaolers

For Imogens deere life, take mine, and though
'Tis not so deere, yet 'tis a life; you coyn'd it,
'Tweene man, and man, they waigh not every stampe:
30   Though light, take Peeces for the figures sake,
(You rather) mine being yours: and so great Powres,
If you will take[1] this Audit, take this life,
And cancell these cold Bonds.
                            Oh Imogen,
35   Ile speake to thee in silence.

**SOLEMNE MUSICKE. ENTER (AS IN AN APPARATION) SICILLIUS LEO-
NATUS, FATHER TO POSTHUMUS, AN OLD MAN, ATTYRED, LIKE A WAR-
RIOUR, LEADING IN HIS HAND AN ANCIENT MATRON (HIS WIFE, &
MOTHER TO POSTHUMUS) WITH MUSICKE BEFORE THEM. THEN,
AFTER OTHER MUSICKE, FOLLOWES THE TWO YOUNG LEONATI (BRO-
THERS TO POSTHUMUS) WITH WOUNDS AS THEY DIED IN THE WARRS.
THEY CIRCLE POSTHUMUS ROUND AS HE LIES SLEEPING [2]**

Sicilius Leonatus   No more thou Thunder-Master/ shew° thy spight, on Mortall Flies:
                      With Mars fall out with Juno chide,° that thy Adulteries
                             Rates, and Revenges.

                     Hath my poore Boy done ought but well,/ whose face I never saw:
40   I dy'de whil'st in the Wombe he staide,/ attending Natures Law.

                     Whose Father then (as men report,/ thou Orphanes Father art)
                     Thou should'st have bin, and sheelded him,/ from this earth-vexing smart.

[W][1] Ff = 'take', some modern texts = 'make' (arguing the 'take' set two words later ('take this life')
     influenced the setting of this word

[F][2] the following Masque has been the subject of much intense questioning with the conclusion often
     reached that it is probably non-Shakespearean: this text supports the arguments of Wilson Knight, Hardin
     Craig, and J. M. Nosworthy (among others) that the passage is essentially Shakespearean and can do no
     better than requote Hardin Craig as already cited in Professor Nosworthy's exemplary introduction to his
     Arden edition of the play (op. cit.)

         All in all, it seems possible to defend the authenticity of the masque and other stylistic
         abnormalities on the ground that gods and those who speak to gods, especially if they
         themselves are spirits, must speak differently from creatures of this world.
               (Hardin Craig, 'Shakespeare's Bad Poetry', Shakespeare Survey, 1, page 55)

Nosworthy goes on to argue that the section is essentially written in the '14-er' rhyme pattern of the 1590's
but unfortunately does not print the complete passage in the main body of the text that way. It is an
excellent argument and, when set out that way on the paper, it is easy to see the 'normal' pattern of
doublets and triplets which are occasionally broken at stressful or ritual moments by shorter lines.

   This edition will take the unusual step of not following the Ff layout but will, instead, follow the Nosworthy
argument. Any changes from Ff lineation will be shown with the symbol '/': (The modern relineation
sometimes follows that of Ff: any common extra deviation will be marked with the symbol °. The
unaltered Ff layout may be found in an Appendix at the end of this script.)

Mother	Lucina lent not me her ayde,/ but tooke me in my Throwes,	
	That from me was Posthumus ript,/ came crying 'mong'st his Foes.	
45	A thing of pitty.	

Sicilius Leonatus	Great Nature like his Ancestrie,/ moulded the stuffe so faire:
	That he deserv'd ^{† 1} the praise o'th'World,/ as great Sicilius heyre.

1st. Brother	When once he was mature for man,/ in Britaine where was hee
	That could stand up his paralell ?/ Or fruitfull object bee?
50	In eye of Imogen, that best° could deeme /his dignitie.

Mother	With Marriage wherefore was he mockt /to be exil'd, and throwne
	From Leonati Seate, and cast° from her,/ his deerest one :
	Sweete Imogen?

Sicilius Leonatus Why did you suffer Iachimo,° slight thing of Italy,   R 393 - b

55 To taint his Nobler hart & braine,° with needlesse jelousy,

  And to become the geeke ² ° and scorne o'th'others vilany ?

2nd. Brother For this, from stiller Seats we came ,/ ³ our Parents, and us twaine,

  That striking in our Countries cause,/ fell bravely, and were slaine,

  Our Fealty, & Tenantius right,° with Honor to maintaine.

60 **1st. Brother** Like hardiment Posthumus /hath to Cymbeline perform'd :

  Then Jupiter, ÿ⁴ King of Gods,° why hast ÿ thus adjourn'd

  The Graces for his Merits due,° being all to dolors turn'd?

Sicilius Leonatus Thy Christall window ope; looke,/ looke out,° no longer exercise

  Upon a valiant Race, thy harsh,° and potent injuries: ⁵

65 **Mother** Since (Jupiter) our Son is good,/ take off his miseries.

Sicilius Leonatus Peepe through thy Marble Mansion, helpe,/ or we poore Ghosts will cry

  To'th'shining Synod of the rest,° against thy Deity .

Brothers Helpe (Jupiter) or we appeale,/ and from thy justice flye.

**JUPITER DESCENDS IN THUNDER AND LIGHTNING, SITTING UPPON AN
EAGLE: HEE THROWES A THUNDER-BOLT. THE GHOSTES FALL ON
THEIR KNEES ⁶**

R 393 - b / L 394 - b : 5.4.43 - 5.4.92

^{W 1} F2 and most modern texts = 'he deserved,' F1 = 'he d serv'd'

^{W 2} Ff = 'geeke', some modern texts = 'geck'

^{W 3} Ff = 'came', some modern texts = 'come'

^{W 4} F1 = 'ÿ', F2/most modern texts = 'thou'

^{PCT 5} Ff set a colon to end the father's plea for society at large, almost as if his wife interrupts him with a
more direct, personal and urgent request for their son: most modern texts set a period

^{STR 6} and now, with the ritual appeal completed, the play's scansion returns to the more normal regular
iambic pentameter and its natural variants

Jupiter	No more you petty Spirits of Region low
70	Offend our hearing: hush.
	How dare you Ghostes
	Accuse the Thunderer, whose Bolt (you know)
	Sky-planted, batters all rebelling Coasts.
	Poore shadowes of Elizium, hence, and rest
75	Upon your never-withering bankes of Flowres.
	Be not with mortall accidents opprest,
	No care of yours it is, you know 'tis ours.
	Whom best I love, I crosse; to make my guift
	The more delay'd, delighted.
80	Be content,
	Your low-laide Sonne, our Godhead will uplift:
	His Comforts thrive, his Trials well are spent:
	Our Joviall Starre reign'd at his Birth, and in
	Our Temple was he married: Rise, and fade,
85	He shall be Lord of Lady Imogen,
	And happier much by his Affliction made.
	This Tablet lay upon his Brest, wherein
	Our pleasure, his full Fortune, doth confine,
	And so away: [1] no farther with your dinne
90	Expresse Impatience, least you stirre up mine:
	Mount Eagle, to my Palace Christalline.

[Ascends]

Sicilius Leonatus	He came in Thunder, his Celestiall breath
	Was sulphurous to smell: the holy Eagle
	Stoop'd, as to foote us: his Ascension is
95	More sweet then our blest Fields: his Royall Bird
	Prunes[2] the immortall wing, and cloyes[3] his Beake,
	As when his God is pleas'd.
	}
All	Thankes Jupiter.
Sicilius Leonatus	The Marble Pavement clozes, he is enter'd
100	His radiant Roofe: Away, and to be blest
	Let us with care performe his great behest. [4]

[Vanish] [5]

SD 1
   some modern texts add a stage direction that the ghosts somehow receive the tablet from Jupiter and
   either here, or more appropriately just before they vanish, give it to or lay it upon the breast of Posthumus

W 2
   Ff = 'Prunes', most modern texts = 'Preens'

W 3
   Ff = 'cloyes', most modern texts = 'claws'

SD 4
   this is where most modern texts place the second part of the direction shown in footnote #1 above

SD 5
   most modern texts explain Posthumus awakes only after they have vanished

Posthumus	Sleepe, thou hast bin a Grandsire, and begot
	A Father to me: and thou hast created
	A Mother, and two Brothers.

105

Gone, they went hence so soone as they were borne:
And so I am awake.
Poore Wretches, that depend
On Greatnesse, Favour; Dreame as I have done,

110 Wake, and finde nothing.
But (alas) I swerve:
Many Dreame not to finde, neither deserve,
And yet are steep'd in Favours; so am I
That have this Golden chance, and know not why:

115 What Fayeries haunt this ground?
A Book?
Oh rare one,   L 394 - b
Be not, as is our fangled world, a Garment
Nobler then that it covers.

120 Let thy effects
So follow, to be most unlike our Courtiers,
As good, as promise.

READES

When[†] as a Lyons whelpe, shall to himselfe unknown, with-
out seeking finde, and bee embrac'd by a peece of tender
125 *Ayre: And when from a stately Cedar shall be lopt branches,*
which being dead many yeares, shall after revive, bee joynted to
the old Stocke, and freshly grow, then shall Posthumus end his
miseries, Britaine be fortunate, and flourish in Peace and Plen-
tie.

130 'Tis still a Dreame: or else such stuffe as madmen
Tongue, and braine not: either both, or nothing,
Or senselesse speaking, or a speaking such
As sense cannot untye.
Be what it is,
135 The Action of my life is like it, which Ile keepe
If but for simpathy.

ENTER GAOLER [1]

| Gaoler | Come Sir, are you ready for death? |
| Posthumus | Over-roasted rather: ready long ago. |

L 394 - b / R 394 - b : 5.4.123 - 5.4.152

[P][1]
as only one Gaoler is given an entry, all modern texts suggest it is the 1st. Gaoler from the
previous scene

Gaoler		Hanging is the word, Sir, if you bee readie for
140		that, you are well Cook'd.
	Posthumus	So if I prove a good repast to the Spectators, the
		dish payes the shot.
	Gaoler	A heavy reckoning for you Sir: But the comfort
		is you shall be called to no more payments, fear no more
145		Taverne Bils, which are ¹ often the sadnesse of parting, as
		the procuring of mirth: you come in faint for want of
		meate, depart reeling with too much drinke: sorrie that
		you have payed too much, and sorry that you are payed
		too much: Purse and Braine, both empty: the Brain the
150		heavier, for being too light; the Purse too light, being
		drawne of heavinesse.

Oh, ² of this contradiction you shall
now be quit: Oh the charity of a penny Cord, it summes
up thousands in a trice: you have no true Debitor, and
Creditor but it: of what's past, is, and to come, the dis-
charge: your necke (Sir†³) is Pen, Booke, and Counters; so
the Acquittance followes.

	Posthumus	I am merrier to dye, then thou art to live.
	Gaoler	Indeed Sir, he that sleepes, feeles not the Tooth-
160		Ache: but a man that were to sleepe your sleepe, and a
		Hangman to helpe him to bed, I think he would change
		places with his Officer: for, look you Sir, you know not
		which way you shall go.
	Posthumus	Yes indeed do I, fellow.
165	**Gaoler**	Your death has eyes in's head then: I have not
		seene him so pictur'd: you must either bee directed by
		some that take upon them to know, or to⁴ take upon your
		selfe that which I am sure you do not know: or jump the
		after-enquiry on your owne perill: and how you shall
170		speed in your journies end, I thinke you'l never returne
		to tell one. ⁵

ᵂ₁ though Ff have no extra words here, some modern texts add the word 'as'

ᵂ₂ some modern texts omit the word 'Oh'

ᵂ₃ F2 and most modern texts = 'Sir', F1 = 'Sis'

ᵂ₄ some modern texts omit the word 'to'

ᵂ₅ Ff = 'one', some modern texts = 'on'

Posthumus	I tell thee, Fellow, there are none want eyes, to direct them the way I am going, but such as winke, and will not use them.	
175 **Gaoler**	What an infinite mocke is this, that a man shold have the best use of eyes, to see the way of blindnesse: I am sure hanging's the way of winking.	

ENTER A MESSENGER

Messenger	Knocke off his Manacles, bring your Prisoner to the King.	
180 **Posthumus**	Thou bring'st good newes, I am call'd to bee made free.	
Gaoler	Ile be hang'd then.	
Posthumus	Thou shalt be then freer then a Gaoler; no bolts for the dead. [1]	R 394 - b
185 **Gaoler**	Unlesse a manwould marry a Gallowes, & be-get yong Gibbets, I never saw one so prone: yet on my Conscience, there are verier Knaves desire to live, for all he be a Roman; and there be some of them too that dye against their willes; so should I, if I were one.	
190	I would we were all of one minde, and one minde good: O there were desolation of Gaolers and Galowses: I speake a-gainst my present profit, but my wish hath a preferment in't.	

[Exeunt]

R 394 - b / L 395 - b : 5.4.185 - 5.4.206

[SD 1] despite the Ff stage direction 'EXEUNT' at the end of the scene, most modern texts give an exit here to both Posthumus and the Messenger

Scena Quinta

[Some modern texts refer to this as Act Five Scene 4]

**ENTER CYMBELINE, BELLARIUS, GUIDERIUS, ARVI-
RAGUS, PISANIO, AND LORDS**

Cymbeline	Stand by my side you, whom the Gods have made
	Preservers of my Throne : woe is my heart,
	That the poore Souldier that so richly fought,
	Whose ragges, sham'd gilded Armes, whose naked brest
	Stept before Targes of proofe, cannot be found :
	He shall be happy that can finde him, if
	Our†¹ Grace can make him so.

}

Belarius	I never saw
	Such Noble fury in so poore a Thing ;
	Such precious deeds, in one that promist nought
	But beggery, and poore lookes.

}

Cymbeline	No tydings of him?

Pisanio	He hath bin search'd among the dead, & living ;
	But no trace of him.

}

Cymbeline	To my greefe, I am
	The heyre of his Reward, which I will adde
	To you² (the Liver, Heart, and Braine of Britaine)
	By whom (I grant) she lives.

'Tis now the time

To aske of whence you are.

Report it. ³

Belarius	Sir,
	In Cambria are we borne, and Gentlemen :
	Further to boast, were neyther true, nor modest,
	Unlesse I adde, we are honest.

L 395 - b : 5.5.1 - 5.5.19

ᵂ ₁ F1 = 'Onr', F2 = 'Our'

ᵂᴴᴼ ₂ most modern texts indicate that Cymbeline is talking to Belarius and the two boys

ᴸˢ ₃ usually modern texts add the one word line 'Sir,' opening Belarius' following long speech, to form a single split line, but it would be worthwhile to explore the Ff layout: the nine syllable line from Cymbeline allows for a tiny pause before having to request more directly 'Report it.", and the inherent pauses of the one syllable line before Belarius starts his somewhat evasive reply could be very effective theatrically

Cymbeline	Bow your knees:
	Arise my Knights o'th'Battell, I create you
	Companions to our person, and will fit you
	With Dignities becomming your estates.

ENTER CORNELIUS AND LADIES

30   There's businesse in these faces: why so sadly
Greet you our Victory? you looke like Romaines,
And not o'th'Court of Britaine.

Cornelius   Hayle great King,
To sowre your happinesse, I must report
35   The Queene is dead.

Cymbeline   Who worse then a Physitian
Would this report become?
                   But I consider,
By Med'cine life may be prolong'd, yet death
40   Will seize the Doctor too.
                       How ended she?

Cornelius   With horror, madly dying, like her life,
Which (being cruell to the world) concluded
Most cruell to her selfe.
45   What she confest,
I will report, so please you.
                   These her Women
Can trip me, if I erre, who with wet cheekes
Were present when she finish'd.

50   **Cymbeline**   Prythee say.

Cornelius   First, she confest she never lov'd you: onely
Affected Greatnesse got by you: not you:
Married your Royalty, was wife to your place: L 395 - b
Abhorr'd your person.

55   **Cymbeline**   She alone knew this:
And but she spoke it dying, I would not
Beleeve her lips in opening it.
                  Proceed.

Cornelius   Your daughter, whom she bore in hand to love
60   With such integrity, she did confesse
Was as a Scorpion to her sight, whose life
(But that her flight prevented it) she had
Tane off by poyson.

Cymbeline	O most delicate Fiend!
65		Who is't can read a Woman?
	Is there more?

Cornelius	More Sir, and worse.
	She did confesse she had
	For you a mortall Minerall, which being tooke,
70		Should by the minute feede on life, and ling'ring,
	By inches waste you.
	In which time, she purpos'd
	By watching, weeping, tendance, kissing, to
	Orecome you with her shew; [1] and in time[2]
75		(When she had fitted[3] you with her craft,[4] to worke
	Her Sonne into th'adoption of the Crowne:
	But fayling of her end by his strange absence,
	Grew shamelesse desperate, open'd (in despight
	Of Heaven, and Men) her purposes: repented
80		The evils she hatch'd, were not effected: so
	Dispayring, dyed.

Cymbeline	Heard you all this, her Women?

La. [5]	We did, so please your Highnesse.

Cymbeline	Mine eyes[6]
85		Were not in fault, for she was beautifull:
	Mine eares that heare[7] her flattery, nor my heart,
	That thought her like her seeming.
	It had beene vicious
	To have mistrusted her: yet (Oh my Daughter)
90		That it was folly in me, thou mayst say,
	And prove it in thy feeling.
	Heaven mend all.

**ENTER LUCIUS, IACHIMO, AND OTHER ROMAN PRISONERS,
LEONATUS BEHIND, AND IMOGEN [8]**

R 395 - b : 5.5.48 - 5.5.68

[W1] to expand the line to pentameter F2 adds 'yes': this is not followed by many texts

[W2] though most modern texts agree with Ff and print this as 'time', one gloss = 'fine' (i.e. 'in summary')

[W3] Ff = 'fitted', some modern texts = 'fit' (to render the line back to pure pentameter)

[PCT4] though opening the line with a bracket, Ff do no set a closing one: most modern texts set one here

[P5] Ff give the prefix 'La.' which could be singular or plural: while many modern texts assign the speech
to all the Ladies, this script will set the Ff prefix and let readers make their own choice

[LS6] traditionally these two words are joined to the previous short line to form a single split verse line:
however, the irrevocable finality of the Lady's reply could well give Cymbeline time to pause before
honestly expressing his most personal of feelings publicly

[W7] F1-2 = 'heare', most modern texts and F3 = 'heard'

[SD8] most modern texts expand the entry to include the Soothsayer and Posthumus, as well as Guards

		Thou comm'st not Caius now for Tribute, that
		The Britaines have rac'd [1] out, though with the losse
95		Of many a bold one: whose Kinsmen have made suite
		That their good soules may be appeas'd, with slaughter
		Of you their Captives, which our selfe have granted,
		So thinke of your estate.

	Lucius	Consider Sir, the chance of Warre, the day
100		Was yours by accident: had it gone with us,
		We should not when the blood was cool, have threatend
		Our Prisoners with the Sword.
		But since the Gods
		Will have it thus, that nothing but our lives
105		May be call'd ransome, let it come: Sufficeth,
		A Roman, with a Romans heart can suffer:
		Augustus lives to thinke on't: and so much
		For my peculiar care.
		This one thing onely
110		I will entreate, [2] my Boy (a Britaine borne)
		Let him be ransom'd: Never Master had
		A Page so kinde, so duteous, diligent,
		So tender over his occasions, true,
		So feate, so Nurse-like: let his vertue joyne
115		With my request, which Ile make bold, your Highnesse
		Cannot deny: he hath done no Britaine harme,
		Though he have serv'd a Roman.
		Save him (Sir)
		And spare no blood beside.
		}

	Cymbeline	I have surely seene him:
120		His favour is familiar to me: Boy,
		Thou hast look'd thy selfe into my grace,
		And art mine owne.
		I know not why, wherefore,
125		To say, live boy: ne're thanke thy Master, live;
		And aske of Cymbeline what Boone thou wilt,
		Fitting my bounty, and thy state, Ile give it:
		Yea, though thou do demand a Prisoner
		The Noblest tane.
		}

| | **Imogen** | I humbly thanke your Highnesse. |

| | **Lucius** | I do not bid thee begge my life, good Lad, |
| | | And yet I know thou wilt. |

R 395 - b

R 395 - b / L 396 - b   :   5.5.69 - 5.5.102

W [1] Ff = 'rac'd', most modern texts = 'raz'd'

SD [2] most modern texts suggest somewhere in this speech that Lucius presents the disguised Imogen to her father

Imogen	No, no, alacke, There's other worke in hand: I see a thing Bitter to me, as death: your life, good Master, Must shuffle for it selfe.	

135

Lucius	The Boy disdaines me, He leaves me, scornes me: briefely dye their joyes, That place them on the truth of Gyrles, and Boyes.

140

Why stands he so perplext?

Cymbeline   What would'st thou Boy?

I love thee more, and more: thinke more and more
What's best to aske.
                            Know'st him thou look'st on? speak

145   Wilt have him live?
                            Is he thy Kin? thy Friend?

Imogen   He is a Romane, no more kin to me,
Then I to your Highnesse, who being born your vassaile
Am something neerer.

150   **Cymbeline**   Wherefore ey'st him so?

Imogen   Ile tell you (Sir) in private, if you please
To give me hearing.

Cymbeline   I, with all my heart,
And lend my best attention.
                            What's thy name?

155

Imogen   Fidele Sir.

Cymbeline   Thou'rt my good youth: my Page
Ile be thy Master: walke with me: speake freely. [1]

Belarius   Is not this Boy reviv'd from death?

160   **Arviragus**   One Sand another[2]
Not more resembles that sweet Rosie Lad: [3]
Who dyed, and was Fidele: what thinke you?

[SD]1 here most modern texts suggest Cymbeline take Imogen aside, freeing the stage for Belarius and the boys

[LS]2 this is often joined to the previous short line to form an overly long single split verse line (thirteen syllables and six strong beats): however, the Ff layout allows a pause for the shock to be felt

[PCT]3 most modern texts seem to regard this colon as ungrammatical and omit it, also replacing the one following with a period,, viz.

    Not more resembles that sweet Rosie Lad/Who dyed, and was Fidele. What thinke you?
thus presenting a fairly rational approach to a highly surprising (and emotional) situation: the Ff setting

    Not more resembles that sweet Rosie Lad: / Who dyed, and was Fidele: what thinke you?
allows both for Arvigarus' surprise and his attempt to preserve rationality

Guiderius		The same dead thing alive.
Belarius	165	Peace, peace, see further: he eyes us not, forbeare[1] Creatures may be alike: were't he, I am sure He would have spoke to us.
Guiderius		But we see him dead.
Belarius		Be silent: let's see further.
Pisanio	170	It is my Mistris: [2] Since she is living, let the time run on, To good, or bad.
Cymbeline		Come, stand thou by our side, Make thy demand alowd. [3] Sir, step you forth,
	175	Give answer to this Boy, and do it freely, Or by our Greatnesse, and the grace of it (Which is our Honor) bitter torture shall Winnow the truth from falshood. One[4] speake to him.
Imogen	180	My boone is, that this Gentleman may render Of whom he had this Ring.
Posthumus		What's that to him? [5]
Cymbeline		That Diamond upon your Finger, say How came it yours?
Iachimo	185	Thou'lt torture me to leave unspoken, that Which to be spoke, wou'd torture thee.
Cymbeline		How? me?
Iachimo	190	I am glad to be constrain'd to utter that Which torments me to conceale. By Villany I got this Ring: 'twas Leonatus Jewell, Whom thou did'st banish: and which more may greeve thee, †

L 396 - b : 5.5.123 - 5.5.144

PCT [1] ending with no punctuation F1 presents another ungrammatical moment, perhaps suggesting Belarius is rushing through trying to keep (his? the boys'?) emotions in check: F2/most modern texts set a comma

A [2] most modern texts indicate this is spoken as an aside

SD [3] most modern texts combine up to three stage directions here: first that Cymbeline and Imogen have come forward; that Cymbeline first talks to Imogen; and that the 'Sir' to step forward is Iachimo

W [4] Ff = 'One', most modern texts = 'On'

A [5] most modern texts indicate this is spoken as an aside

128

As it doth me: a Nobler Sir ne're liv'd
'Twixt sky and ground.
195   Wilt thou heare more my Lord?

Cymbeline   All that belongs to this.

Iachimo   That Paragon, thy daughter,
For whom my heart drops blood, and my false spirits
Quaile to remember.
200   Give me leave, I faint.

Cymbeline   My Daughter? what of hir?
                Renew thy strength[1]   L 396 - b
I had rather thou should'st live, while Nature will,
Then dye ere I heare more: strive man, and speake.

205   **Iachimo**   Upon a time, unhappy was the clocke
That strooke the houre: it was in Rome, accurst
The Mansion where: 'twas at a Feast, oh would
Our Viands had bin poyson'd (or at least
Those which I heav'd to head:) the good Posthumus,
210   (What should I say? he was too good to be
Where ill men were, and was the best of all
Among'st the rar'st of good ones) sitting sadly,
Hearing us praise our Loves of Italy
For Beauty, that made barren the swell'd boast
215   Of him that best could speake: for Feature, laming
The Shrine of Venus, or straight-pight Minerva,
Postures, beyond breefe Nature.
                      For Condition,
A shop of all the qualities, that man
220   Loves woman for, besides that hooke of Wiving,
Fairenesse, which strikes the eye.

Cymbeline   I stand on fire. °
               Come to the matter.
Iachimo   All too soone I shall,° [2]
225   Unlesse thou would'st greeve quickly.
                      This Posthumus,
Most like a Noble Lord, in love, and one
That had a Royall Lover, tooke his hint,
And (not dispraising whom we prais'd, therein
230   He was as calme as vertue) he began

L 396 - b / R 396 - b : 5.5.145 - 5.5.174

[PCT 1] neither F1 nor F2 show any punctuation here - allowing for Cymbeline's passionate onrush: most
modern texts are forced to set some form of punctuation for grammatical purposes

[LS 2] most modern texts take away the pauses from Iachimo (which build Cymbeline's anxiety even further)
by reducing three irregular Ff lines (6/9/5 syllables) to two regular pentameter lines as shown (°)

His Mistris picture, which, by his tongue, being made,
And then a minde put in't, either our bragges
Were crak'd of Kitchin-Trulles, or his description
Prov'd us unspeaking sottes.

235	**Cymbeline**	Nay, nay, to'th'purpose.
	Iachimo	Your daughters Chastity, (there it beginnes)

He spake of her, as Dian had hot dreames,
And she alone, were cold: Whereat, I wretch
Made scruple of his praise, and wager'd with him

240   Peeces of Gold, 'gainst this, which then he wore
Upon his honour'd finger) to attaine
In suite the place of's bed, and winne this Ring,
By hers, and mine Adultery: he (true Knight)
No lesser of her Honour confident

245   Then I did truly finde her, stakes this Ring,
And would so, had it beene a Carbuncle
Of Phœbus Wheele; and might so safely, had it
Bin all the worth of's Carre.

                        Away to Britaine

250   Poste I in this designe: Well may you (Sir)
Remember me at Court, where I was taught
Of your chaste Daughter, the wide difference
'Twixt Amorous, and Villanous.

                        Being thus quench'd

255   Of hope, not longing; mine Italian braine,
Gan in your duller Britaine operare[1]
Most vildely: for my vantage excellent.

And to be breefe, my practise so prevayl'd
That I return'd with simular proofe enough,

260   To make the Noble Leonatus mad,
By wounding his beleefe in her Renowne,
With Tokens thus, and thus: averring notes
Of Chamber-hanging, Pictures, this her Bracelet
(Oh cunning how I got[2]) nay some markes

265   Of secret on her person, that he could not
But thinke her bond of Chastity quite crack'd,
I having 'tane the forfeyt.

                        Whereupon,
Me thinkes I see him now.

270	**Posthumus**	I so thou do'st,[3]

[W1] F1 = 'operare', F2 and most modern texts = 'operate'

[W2] though Ff have no extra words here, some modern texts add the word 'it' to extend the line to pentameter

[SD3] most modern texts add the stage direction that Posthumus reveals himself and/or advances

Italian Fiend.

        Aye me, most credulous Foole,
Egregious murtherer, Theefe, any thing
That's due to all the Villaines past, in being
275   To come.   R 396 - b
                Oh give me Cord, or knife, or poyson,
Some upright Justicer.
                            Thou King, send out
For Torturors ingenious : it is I
280   That all th'abhorred things o'th'earth amend
By being worse then they.
                      I am Posthumus,
That kill'd thy Daughter : Villain-like, I lye,
That caus'd a lesser villaine then my selfe,
285   A sacrilegious Theefe to doo't.
                         The Temple
Of Vertue was she ; yea, and she her selfe.

Spit, and throw stones, cast myre upon me, set
The dogges o'th'street to bay me : every villaine
290   Be call'd Posthumus Leonatus , and
Be villany[1] lesse then 'twas.
                      Oh Imogen!
My Queene, my life, my wife : oh Imogen,
Imogen, Imogen.   }

295   **Imogen**   Peace my Lord, heare, heare.

Posthumus	Shall's have a play of this?
	Thou scornfull Page,° there lye thy part.
Pisanio	Oh Gentlemen, helpe,° [2]

                 Mine and your Mistris : Oh my Lord Posthumus,
300   You ne're kill'd Imogen till now : helpe, helpe,
                 Mine honour'd Lady.   }

Cymbeline   Does the world go round? }

Posthumus   How comes these staggers on mee?
                               }

Pisanio   Wake my Mistris.

R 396 - b / L 397 - b : 5.5.210 - 5.5.233

[W][1] Ff = 'villany', some texts = 'villaine'

[LS][2] modern texts usually reduce the three irregular Ff lines (6/8/5 syllables) to two almost metrically
correct lines (10/9) but, again, in so doing they tend to spoil the impact of the stage directions they have
added in, first that Imogen rushes to Posthumus and that he, not knowing it is her, throws her aside (some
texts go so far as to give the direction that he hits her or strikes her down though such blatantly deliberate
action is not so directed in the original scripts) and, secondly, that then Pisanio comes forward

305	**Cymbeline**	If this be so, the Gods do meane to strike me
		To death, with mortall joy.
	Pisanio	How fares my Mistris?
	Imogen	Oh get thee from my sight,[1]
		Thou gav'st me poyson: dangerous Fellow hence,
310		Breath not where Princes are.
	Cymbeline	The tune of Imogen.
	Pisanio	Lady, the Gods throw stones of sulpher on me, if
		That box I gave you, was not thought by mee
		A precious thing, I had it from the Queene.
315	**Cymbeline**	New matter still.
	Imogen	It poyson'd me.
	Cornelius	Oh Gods!
		I left out one thing which the Queene confest,
		Which must approve thee honest.
320		If Pisanio[†2]
		Have (said she) given his Mistris that Confection
		Which I gave him for Cordiall, she is serv'd,
		As I would serve a Rat.
	Cymbeline	What's this, Cornelius ?
325	**Cornelius**	The Queene (Sir) very oft importun'd me
		To temper poysons for her, still pretending
		The satisfaction of her knowledge, onely
		In killing Creatures vilde, as Cats and Dogges
		Of no esteeme.
330		I dreading, that her purpose
		Was of more danger, did compound for her
		A certaine stuffe, which being tane, would cease
		The present powre of life, but in short time,
		All Offices of Nature, should againe
335		Do their due Functions.
		Have you tane of it?
	Imogen	Most like I did, for I was dead.
	Belarius	My Boyes,° there was our error.

[SP][1] the actor has choice as to which two of these three short lines may be joined as one line of split verse

[W][2] F2 and most modern texts = 'Pisanio', F1 = 'Pasanio'

Guiderius	This is sure Fidele. ° ¹
340 **Imogen**	Why did you throw your wedded Lady fro² you?
	Thinke that you are upon a Rocke, and now
	Throw me againe.
Posthumus	Hang there like fruite, my soule,
	Till the Tree dye.
345 **Cymbeline**	How now, my Flesh? my Childe?
	What, mak'st thou me a dullard in this Act?
	Wilt thou not speake to me?
Imogen	Your blessing, Sir.
Belarius	Though you° did love this youth, I blame ye not,° ³ 397-b
350	You had a motive for't.
Cymbeline	My teares that fall
	Prove holy-water on thee; Imogen,
	Thy Mothers dead.
Imogen	I am sorry for't, my Lord.
355 **Cymbeline**	Oh, she was naught; and long of her it was
	That we meet heere so strangely: but her Sonne
	Is gone, we know not how, nor where.
Pisanio	My Lord,
	Now feare is from me, Ile speake troth.
360	Lord Cloten
	Upon my Ladies missing, came to me
	With his Sword drawne, foam'd at the mouth, and swore
	If I discover'd not which way she was gone,
	It was my instant death.
365	By accident,
	I had a feigned Letter of my Masters
	Then in my pocket, which directed him
	To seeke her on the Mountaines neere to Milford,
	Where in a frenzie, in my Masters Garments

L 397 - b / R 397 - b : 5.5.260 - 5.5.282

^LS1 by invoking the argument of white space to reduce the three Ff short lines (8/7/5 or 6) to two almost
pure pentameter (10/10 or 11), the modern texts once again have eradicated pauses useful for the various
momentary on-stage reactions to a fresh series of shocks and delights: this occurs at least five more times
in the scene and, for brevity, each occurrence will be referred back to this footnote

^W2 Ff = 'fro', most modern texts = 'from'

^LS3 this is the second 'shock/delight' Ff irregularity, see footnote #1 above

370   (Which he inforc'd from me) away he postes
    With unchaste purpose, and with oath to violate
    My Ladies honor, what became of him,

    I further know not.

Guiderius   Let me end the Story: I slew him there.

375   **Cymbeline**   Marry, the Gods forefend. [1]

    I would not thy good deeds, should from my lips
    Plucke a hard sentence: Prythee valiant youth

    Deny't againe.

Guiderius   I have spoke it, and I did it.

380   **Cymbeline**   He was a Prince. [2]

Guiderius   A most incivill one.
                   The wrongs he did mee
    Were nothing Prince-like; for he did provoke me
    With Language that would make me spurne the Sea,

385   If it could so roare to me.
                    I cut off's head,
    And am right glad he is not standing heere
    To tell this tale of mine.
                            }

Cymbeline   I am sorrow for thee:

390   By thine owne tongue thou art condemn'd, and must

    Endure our Law: Thou'rt dead.

Imogen   That headlesse man° I thought had bin my Lord [3]

Cymbeline   Binde the Offender, ° [4]

    And take him from our presence.
                           }

395   **Belarius**   Stay, Sir King.

    This man[5] is better then the man he slew,
    As well descended as thy selfe, and hath
    More of thee merited, then a Band of Clotens
    Had ever scarre for.

LS[1] this is the third 'shock/delight' Ff irregularity, , see footnote #1 on the previous page

LS[2] the actor has choice as to which two of these three short lines may be joined as one line of split verse

PCT[3] as Ff offer no punctuation here it could be as if Cymbeline was interrupting her; most modern texts
finish the sentence with a period

LS[4] this is the fourth 'shock/delight' Ff irregularity, see footnote #1 on this and the previous page

W[5] Ff = 'man', some texts = 'youth' or 'boy'

400		Let his Armes alone,[1]
		They were not borne for bondage.
	Cymbeline	Why old Soldier:
		Wilt thou undoo the worth thou art unpayd for
		By tasting of our wrath?
405		How of descent
		As good as we?
	Arviragus	In that he spake too farre.
	Cymbeline	And thou shalt dye for't.
	Belarius	We will dye all three,
410		But I will prove that two one's[2] are as good
		As I have given out him.
		My Sonnes, I must
		For mine owne part, unfold a dangerous speech,
		Though haply well for you.
415	**Arviragus**	Your danger's ours.
	Guiderius	And our good his.
	Belarius	Have at it then, by leave
		Thou hadd'st (great King) a Subject, who

Was call'd Belarius.

420	**Cymbeline**	What of him?
		He is° a banish'd Traitor.
	Belarius	He it is, that hath° [3]

Assum'd this age: indeed a banish'd man,
I know not how, a Traitor.

R 397 - b

425	**Cymbeline**	Take him hence
		The whole world shall not save him.
	Belarius	Not too hot;
		First pay me for the Nursing of thy Sonnes,
		And let it be confiscate all, so soone
430		As I have receyv'd it.
	Cymbeline	Nursing of my Sonnes?

R 397 - b / L 398 - b : 5.5.305 - 5.5.322

[SD1] most modern texts have this addressed to whomever it is presumed to have hold of Guiderius at this time, normally one or more of the Guards who have been watching over the Roman prisoners

[W2] F1 -2 = 'one's', F3 and most modern texts = 'on's'

[LS3] this is the fifth 'shock/delight' Ff irregularity, ee footnote #1 on the two previous pages

Belarius		I am too blunt, and sawcy: heere's my knee: [1]
		Ere I arise, I will preferre my Sonnes,
		Then spare not the old Father.
435		Mighty Sir,
		These two young Gentlemen that call me Father,
		And thinke they are my Sonnes, are none of mine,
		They are the yssue of your Loynes, my Liege,
		And blood of your begetting.

}

440 **Cymbeline**   How? my Issue.

Belarius   So sure as you, your Fathers: I (old Morgan)
Am that Belarius, whom you sometime banish'd:
Your pleasure was my neere[2] offence, my punishment
It selfe, and all my Treason that I suffer'd,
445 Was all the harme I did.
                    These gentle Princes
(For such, and so they are) these twenty yeares
Have I train'd up; those Arts they have, as I
Could put into them.
450   My breeding was (Sir)
As your Highnesse knowes: Their Nurse Euriphile
(Whom for the Theft I wedded) stole these Children
Upon my Banishment: I moov'd her too't,
Having receyv'd the punishment before
455 For that which I did then.
                    Beaten for Loyaltie,
Excited me to Treason.
                    Their deere losse,
The more of you 'twas felt, the more it shap'd
460 Unto my end of stealing them.
                    But gracious Sir,
Heere are your Sonnes againe, and I must loose
Two of the sweet'st Companions in the World.

465 The benediction of these covering Heavens
Fall on their heads like[†3] dew, for they are worthie
To in-lay Heaven with Starres.

}

Cymbeline   Thou weep'st, and speak'st:
The Service that you three have done is more
470 Unlike, then this thou tell'st.
                    I lost my Children,

[SD 1] most modern texts give the direction for him to kneel here, but vary enormously as to when he rises

[W 2] Ff = 'neere', some modern texts = 'meere'

[W 3] F2 and most modern texts = 'like', F1 = 'liks'

	If these be they, I know not how to wish A payre of worthier Sonnes.
Belarius	Be pleas'd awhile; This Gentleman, whom I call Polidore, Most worthy Prince, as yours, is true Guiderius: This Gentleman, my Cadwall, Arviragus.
	Your yonger Princely Son, he Sir, was lapt In a most curious Mantle, wrought by th'hand Of his Queene Mother, which for more probation I can with ease produce.
Cymbeline	Guiderius had Upon his necke a Mole, a sanguine Starre, It was a marke of wonder.
Belarius	This is he, Who hath upon him still that naturall stampe: It was wise Natures end, in the donation To be his evidence now.
Cymbeline	Oh, what am I A Mother to the byrth of three?

475

480

485

490

Nere Mother
Rejoyc'd deliverance more: Blest, pray you be,
That after this strange starting from your Orbes,
You may reigne in them now: Oh Imogen,
Thou hast lost by this a Kingdome.

495 **Imogen** No, my Lord:
I have got two Worlds by't.

Oh my gentle Brothers,
Have we thus met?

Oh never say heereafter   L 398 - b
500 But I am truest speaker.

You call'd me Brother
When I was but your Sister: I you Brothers,
When we[1] were so indeed.

Cymbeline	Did you ere meete?
Arviragus	I my good Lord.
Guiderius	And at first meeting lov'd, Continew'd so, untill we thought he dyed.

505

L 398 - b / R 398 - b   :   5.5.355 - 5.5.380

[W][1] Ff = 'we', some modern texts = 'ye'

	Cornelius	By the Queenes Dramme she swallow'd.

}

510	**Cymbeline**	O rare instinct!

When shall I heare all through?
                              This fierce abridgement,
Hath to it Circumstantiall branches, which
Distinction should be rich in.

515   Where? how liv'd you?

And when came you to serve our Romane Captive?
How parted with your Brother? [1]
                              How first met them?

Why fled you from the Court?

520   And whether these?

And your three motives to the Battaile? with
I know not how much more should be demanded,
And all the other by-dependances
From chance to chance? [2]

525   But not the Time, nor Place
Will serve our long Interrogatories. [3]
                              See, [4]
Posthumus Anchors upon Imogen;
And she (like harmlesse Lightning) throwes her eye
530 On him: her Brothers, Me: [5] her Master hitting
Each object with a Joy: the Counter-change
Is severally in all.
                              Let's quit this ground,
And smoake the Temple with our Sacrifices.

535 Thou art my Brother, [6] so wee'l hold thee ever.

	Imogen	You are my Father too, and did releeve me:

To see this gracious season.

}

R 398 - b : 5.5.381- 5.5.401

[W1] Ff = 'Brother', most modern texts = 'Brothers'

[PCT2] Ff show Cymbeline still in a questioning, emotional and non-grammatical mood: most modern texts make two substantial alterations to the queenes passage, first, by transferring the first two words 'And whether' to the end of the previous sentence, and second, removing all the question marks: this creates a much more rational Cymbeline than was originally shown

[W3] Ff = 'Interrogatories', most modern texts = 'Intergatories' - so the pentameter is faithfully preserved

[SD4] some modern texts provide stage directions to cover all or some of the following described actions

[PCT5] again Ff show emotion swamping Cymbeline with an ungrammatical colon here, and no punctuation after the next phrase 'her Master': most modern texts create a more coherent Cymbeline by replacing the colon with a comma, and adding a second one after 'Master'

[WHO6] as some modern texts indicate, this is said to Belarius, as are Imogen's next lines

Cymbeline	All ore-joy'd
	Save these in bonds, let them be joyfull too,
	For they shall taste our Comfort.
540 **Imogen**	My good Master,° I will yet do you service.
Lucius	Happy be you. ° ¹

Cymbeline	The forlorne Souldier, that so⁺² Nobly fought
	He would have well becom'd this place, and grac'd
	The thankings of a King.
	}
545 **Posthumus**	I am Sir
	The Souldier that did company these three
	In poore beseeming: 'twas a fitment for
	The purpose I then follow'd.
	That I was he,
550	Speake Iachimo , I had you downe, and might
	Have made you finish.
	}
Iachimo	I am downe againe: ³
	But now my heavie Conscience sinkes my knee,
	As then your force did.
555	Take that life, beseech you
	Which I so often owe: but your Ring first,
	And heere the Bracelet of the truest Princesse
	That ever swore her Faith.
	}
Posthumus	Kneele not to me:
560	The powre that I have on you, is to spare you:
	The malice towards you, to forgive you.
	Live
	And deale with others better.
	}
Cymbeline	Nobly doom'd:
565	Wee'l learne our Freenesse of a Sonne-in-Law:
	Pardon's the word to all.
	}
Arviragus	You holpe us Sir,,⁴
	As you did meane indeed to be our Brother,
	Joy'd are we, that you are.
570 **Posthumus**	Your Servant Princes.

R 398 - b : 5.5.401 - 5.5.425

ᴸˢ₁ this is the sixth 'shock/delight' Ff irregularity, the possible reaction from the Lucius pause could be splendid

ᵂ₂ F2 and most modern texts = 'so', F1 = 'no'

ˢᴰ₃ most modern texts sensibly suggest that here Iachimo kneels: some suggest that Posthumus raises

him as he starts his own speech (though judging by his dialogue such a response may be a little romantic)

ᵂᴴᴼ₄ most modern texts indicate that this is spoken to Posthumus

Good my Lord of Rome
Call forth your Sooth-sayer: As I slept, me thought
Great Jupiter upon his Eagle back'd
Appear'd to me, with other sprightly shewes
575 Of mine owne Kindred.
When I wak'd, I found
This Labell on my bosome; whose containing
Is so from sense in hardnesse, that I can   R 398 - b
Make no Collection of it.
580 Let him shew
His skill in the construction.
}

Lucius   Philarmonus.

Soothsayer   Heere, my good Lord.
}

Lucius   Read, and declare the meaning.

READES [1]

585 *WHen as a Lyons whelpe, shall to himselfe unknown, with-*
out seeking finde, and bee embrac'd by a peece of tender
Ayre: And when from a stately Cedar shall be lopt branches,
which being dead many yeares, shall after revive, bee joynted to
the old Stocke, and freshly grow, then shall Posthumus end his
590 *miseries, Britaine be fortunate, and flourish in Peace and Plen-*
tie.

Thou Leonatus art the Lyons Whelpe,
The fit and apt Construction of thy name
Being Leonatus, doth import so much:
595 The peece of tender Ayre, [2] thy vertuous Daughter,
Which we call *Mollis Aer*, and *Mollis Aer*
We terme it *Mulier* ; which *Mulier* I divine
Is this most constant Wife, who even now
Answering the Letter of the Oracle,
600 Unknowne to you unsought, were clipt about
With this most tender Aire.
}

Cymbeline   This hath some seeming.

Soothsayer   The lofty Cedar, Royall Cymbeline
Personates thee: And thy lopt Branches, point
605 Thy two Sonnes forth: who by Belarius stolne
For many yeares thought dead, are now reviv'd
To the Majesticke Cedar joyn'd; whose Issue   L 993 - b[3]

R 398 - b / L 993 - b : 5.5.425 - 5.5.457

[P] [1] Ff do not indicate who reads/interprets the prophecy: from lines 582-4 modern texts choose the Soothsayer

[WHO] [2] modern texts direct the Soothsayer to address this to Cymbeline

[COMP] [3] a compositor error in F1: it may have felt like page 993 was being set, but it should have read 399

Promises Britaine, Peace and Plenty.
)

Cymbeline   Well,
610   My Peace we will begin: And Caius Lucius,
Although the Victor, we submit to Cæsar,
And to the Romane Empire; promising
To pay our wonted Tribute, from the which
We were disswaded by our wicked Queene,
615   Whom heavens in Justice both on her, and hers,
Have laid most heavy hand.

Soothsayer   The fingers of the Powres above, do tune
The harmony of this Peace: the Vision
Which I made knowne to Lucius ere the stroke
620   Of yet this[1] scarse-cold-Battaile, at this instant
Is full accomplish'd.
For the Romaine Eagle
From South to West, on wing soaring aloft
Lessen'd her selfe, and in the Beames o'th'Sun
625   So vanish'd; which fore-shew'd our Princely Eagle
Th'Imperiall Cæsar , should againe unite
His Favour, with the Radiant Cymbeline,
Which shines heere in the West.
)

Cymbeline   Laud we the gods,
630   And let our crooked Smoakes climbe to their Nostrils
From our blest Altars.
Publish we this Peace
To all our Subjects.
Set we forward: Let
635   A Roman, and a Brittish Ensigne wave
Friendly together: so through Luds-Towne march,
And in the Temple of great Jupiter
Our Peace wee'l ratifie: Seale it with Feasts.

Set on there: Never was a Warre did cease
640   (Ere bloodie hands were wash'd) with such a Peace.

EXEUNT

FINIS

W [1] F1-2 = 'yet this', F3 and most modern texts = 'this yet'

COMP [2] a compositor error in F1: it should read 399

APPENDIX A
THE UNEASY RELATIONSHIP OF FOLIO, QUARTOS, AND MODERN TEXTS

Between the years 1590 and 1611, one William Shakespeare, a playwright and actor, delivered to the company of which he was a major shareholder at least thirty-seven plays in handwritten manuscript form. Since the texts belonged to the company upon delivery, he derived no extra income from publishing them. Indeed, as far as scholars can establish, he took no interest in the publication of his plays.

Consequently, without his supervision, yet during his lifetime and shortly after, several different publishers printed eighteen of these plays, each in separate editions. Each of these texts, known as **'Quartos'** because of the page size and method of folding each printed sheet, was about the size of a modern hardback novel. In 1623, seven years after Shakespeare's death, Heminges and Condell, two friends, theatrical colleagues, actors, and fellow shareholders in the company, passed on to the printer, William Jaggard, the handwritten copies of not only these eighteen plays but a further eighteen, of which seventeen had been performed but not yet seen in print.[1] These thirty-six plays were issued in one large volume, each page about the size of a modern legal piece of paper. Anything printed in this larger format was known as 'folio', again because of the page size and the method of sheet folding. Thus the 1623 printing of the collected works is known as **the First Folio,** its 1632 reprint (with more than 1600 unauthorised corrections) the Second Folio, and the next reprint, the 1666 Third Folio, added the one missing play, *Pericles* (which had been set in quarto and performed).

The handwritten manuscript used for the copies of the texts from which both Quartos and the First Folio were printed came from a variety of sources. Closest to Shakespeare were those in his own hand, known as the 'foul papers' because of the natural blottings, crossings out, and corrections. Sometimes he had time to pass the material on to a manuscript copyist who would make a clean copy, known as the 'fair papers'. Whether fair (if there was sufficient time) or foul (if the performance deadline was close), the papers would be passed on to the Playhouse, where a 'Playhouse copy' would be made, from which the 'sides' (individual copies of each part with just a single cue line) would be prepared for each actor. Whether Playhouse copy, fair papers, or foul, the various Elizabethan and Jacobean handwritten manuscripts from which the quartos and Folio came have long since disappeared.

The first printed texts of the Shakespeare plays were products of a speaking-

---

[1] Though written between 1605–09, *Timon of Athens* was not performed publicly until 1761.

hearing society. They were based on rhetoric, a verbal form of arranging logic and argument in a persuasive, pleasing, and entertaining fashion so as to win personal and public debates, a system which allowed individuals to express at one and the same time the steppingstones in an argument while releasing the underlying emotional feelings that accompanied it.[2] Naturally, when ideas were set on paper they mirrored this same form of progression in argument and the accompanying personal release, allowing both neat and untidy thoughts to be seen at a glance (see the General Introduction, pp. xvi–xxi). Thus what was set on paper was not just a silent debate. It was at the same time a reminder of how the human voice might be heard both logically and passionately in that debate.

Such reminders did not last into the eighteenth century. Three separate but interrelated needs insisted on cleaning up the original printings so that silent and speaking reader alike could more easily appreciate the beauties of one of England's greatest geniuses.

First, by 1700, publishing's main thrust was to provide texts to be read privately by people of taste and learning. Since grammar was now the foundation for all writing, publication, and reading, all the Elizabethan and early Jacobean material still based on rhetoric appeared at best archaic and at worst incomprehensible. All printing followed the new universality of grammatical and syntactical standards, standards which still apply today. Consequently any earlier book printed prior to the establishment of these standards had to be reshaped in order to be understood. And the Folio/Quarto scripts, even the revamped versions which had already begun to appear, presented problems in this regard, especially when dealing in the moments of messy human behaviour. Thus, while the first texts were reshaped according to the grammatical knowledge of the 1700s, much of the shaping of the rhetoric was (inadvertently) removed from the plays.

Secondly, the more Shakespeare came to be recognized as a literary poet rather than as a theatrical genius, the less the plays were likely to be considered as performance texts. Indeed plot lines of several of his plays were altered (or ignored) to satisfy the more refined tastes of the period. And the resultant demands for poetic and literary clarity, as well as those of grammar, altered the first printings even further.

Thirdly, scholars argued a need for revision of both Quarto and Folio texts because of 'interfering hands' (hands other than Shakespeare's) having had undue influence on the texts. No matter whether foul or fair papers or Playhouse copy, so the

---

[2]   For an extraordinarily full analysis of the art of rhetoric, readers are guided to Sister Miriam Joseph, *Shakespeare's Use of the Arts of Language* (New York: Haffner Publishing Co., 1947). For a more theatrical overview, readers are directed to Bertram Joseph, *Acting Shakespeare* (New York: Theatre Arts Books, 1960). For an overview involving aspects of Ff/Qq, readers are immodestly recommended to Neil Freeman, *Shakespeare's First Texts*, op. cit.

argument ran, several intermediaries would be involved between Shakespeare's writing of the plays and the printing of them. If the fair papers provided the source text, a copyist might add some peculiarities, as per the well documented Ralph Crane.[3] If the Playhouse copy was the source text, extra information, mainly stage directions, would have been added by someone other than Shakespeare, turning the play from a somewhat literary document into a performance text. Finally, while more than five different compositors were involved in setting the First Folio, five did the bulk of the printing house work: each would have their individual pattern of typesetting—compositor E being singled out as far weaker than the rest. Thus between Shakespeare and the printed text might lie the hand(s) of as few as one and as many as three other people, even more when more than one compositor set an individual play. Therefore critics argue because there is the chance of so much interference between Shakespearean intent and the first printings of the plays, the plays do not offer a stylistic whole, i.e., while the words themselves are less likely to be interfered with, their shapings, the material consistently altered in the early 1700s, are not that of a single hand, and thus cannot be relied upon.

These well-intentioned grammatical and poetic alterations may have introduced Shakespeare to a wider reading audience, but their unforeseen effect was to remove the Elizabethan flavour of argument and of character development (especially in the areas of stress and the resulting textual irregularities), thus watering down and removing literally thousands of rhetorical and theatrical clues that those first performance scripts contained. And it is from this period that the division between ancient and modern texts begins. As a gross generalisation, the first texts, the First Folio and the quartos, could be dubbed 'Shakespeare for the stage'; the second, revamped early 1700 texts 'Shakespeare for the page'.

And virtually all current editions are based on the page texts of the early 1700s. While the words of each play remain basically the same, what shapes them, their sentences, punctuation, spelling, capitalisation, and sometimes even line structure, is often altered, unwittingly destroying much of their practical theatrical value.

It is important to neither condemn the modern editions nor blindly accept the authority of the early stage texts as gospel. This is not a case of 'old texts good, so modern texts bad'. The modern texts are of great help in literary and historical research, especially as to the meanings of obscure words and phrases, and in explaining literary allusions and historical events. They offer guidance to alternative text

---

[3] Though not of the theatre (his principle work was to copy material for lawyers) Crane was involved in the preparation of at least five plays in the Folio, as well as two plays for Thomas Middleton. Scholars characterise his work as demonstrating regular and careful scene and act division, though he is criticised for his heavy use of punctuation and parentheses, apostrophes and hyphens, and 'massed entry' stage directions, i.e. where all the characters with entrances in the scene are listed in a single direction at the top of the scene irrespective of where they are supposed to enter.

readings made by reputed editors, plus sound grammatical readings of difficult passages and clarification of errors that appear in the first printings.[4] In short, they can give the starting point of the play's journey, an understanding of the story, and the conflict between characters within the story. But they can only go so far.

They cannot give you fully the conflict within each character, the very essence for the fullest understanding of the development and resolution of any Shakespeare play. Thanks to their rhetorical, theatrical base the old texts add this vital extra element. They illustrate with great clarity the 'ever-changing present' (see p. xvi in the General Introduction) in the intellectual and emotional life of each character; their passages of harmony and dysfunction, and transitions between such passages; the moments of their personal costs or rewards; and their sensual verbal dance of debate and release. In short, the old texts clearly demonstrate the essential elements of living, breathing, reacting humanity—especially in times of joyous or painful stress.

By presenting the information contained in the First Folio, together with modern restructurings, both tested against theatrical possibilities, these texts should go far in bridging the gap between the two different points of view.

---

[4]   For example, the peculiar phrase 'a Table of greene fields' assigned to Mistress Quickly in describing the death of Falstaffe, *Henry V* (Act Two, Scene 3), has been superbly diagnosed as a case of poor penmanship being badly transcribed: the modern texts wisely set 'a babbled of green fields' instead.

NEIL FREEMAN trained as an actor at the Bristol Old Vic Theatre School. He has acted and directed in England, Canada, and the USA. Currently he is an Head of Graduate Directing and Senior Acting Professor in the Professional Training Programme of the Department of Theatre, Film, and Creative Writing at the University of British Columbia. He also teaches regularly at the National Theatre School of Canada, Concordia University, Brigham Young University in both Provo and Hawaii, and is on the teaching faculty of professional workshops in Montreal, Toronto and Vancouver. He is associated with Shakespeare & Co. in Lenox; the Will Geer Theatre in Los Angeles; Bard on the Beach in Vancouver; Repercussion Theatre in Montreal; and has worked with the Stratford Festival, Canada, and Shakespeare Santa Cruz.

His ground breaking work in using the first printings of the Shakespeare texts in performance, on the rehearsal floor and in the classroom has lead to lectures at the Shakespeare Association of America and workshops at both the ATHE and VASTA, and grants/fellowships from the National Endowment of the Arts (USA), The Social Science and Humanities Research Council (Canada), and York University in Toronto.

His three collations of Shakespeare and music - *A Midsummer Nights Dream* (for three actors, chorus, and Orchestra); *If This Be Love* (for three actors, mezzo-soprano, and Orchestra); *The Four Seasons of Shakespeare and Vivaldi* (for two actors, violin soloist and Chamber Orchestra) - commissioned and performed by Bard On The Beach and The Vancouver Symphony Orchestra have been received with great public acclaim.

SHAKESPEARE'S FIRST TEXTS
by Neil Freeman

"THE ACTOR'S BEST CHAMPION OF THE
FOLIO"　　　　　—Kristin Linklater
　　　　　author of *Freeing Shakespeare's Voice*

Neil Freeman provides students, scholars, theatre-lovers, and, most importantly, actors and directors, with a highly readable, illuminating, and indispensable guide to William Shakespeare's own first quill-inscribed texts — SHAKESPEARE'S FIRST TEXTS.

Four hundred years later, most of the grammatical and typographical information conveyed by this representation in Elizabethan type by the first play compositors has been lost. Or, rather, discarded, in order to conform to the new standards of usage. Granted, this permitted more readers access to Shakespeare's writing, but it also did away with some of Shakespeare himself.

ISBN 1–155783–335–4